CRO

EMERGENCY PREPAREDNESS
MADE EASY

By: Pam Crockett

Cover Photo by: Scott Smith Photography
                         Orem, Utah

Layout by: Les Hooper

Davy the Raccoon "Logos for this book" created by: Sean Hunt

Editing by: Pam & Lonnie Crockett

Compiled by: Pam & Lonnie Crockett

                      Lonnie Crockett - prepared & researched
                      for Corners (Chapters 4, 6, 8, 9, & 10)

Printed in the United States

1st Printing © 2008 by Crockett's Corner

Crocketts Corner LLC   Printed by:
PO Box 508   DMT Publishing
Huntsville, UT 844317   900 North 400 West #12
www.crockettscorner.com   North Salt Lake, UT
pam@crockettscorner.com   84054

INTRODUCTION

Preparedness is preparing for the unexpected. It is
a practice of being aware and alert to the possible
and probable reality of a disaster happening at
some time in the future. This important book came
by way of my husband, Lonnie, living through the
Great Alaskan earthquake in 1964, and because of
parents who were prepared for disaster, comfort was
felt by not only the family, but neighbors and friends
whom they helped. What a comfort that must be.
Somehow, we have gotten away from the mind set
of preparing for unforseen problems. We have been
lulled into a false sense of security. If normal
distribution of food to the grocery stores was curtailed,
what sources of food would you have available to you
and your family? If electricity were to be unavailable
for an extended period of time, what methods would
you use for cooking, heating or lighting your home?
If you had to evacuate your home, where would you
go for shelter? The unforseen can come from
natural disasters, man-caused disasters, personal
or community disasters. This book was written and
compiled to help understand the importance of
preparedness and how easy you can establish a plan for
your family. Your efforts will be blessed. I hope you
enjoy this book.

DEDICATION

To families struggling to figure out what to do and how to go about getting prepared for Emergencies and the all too critical food and water storage. May you have fun learning new ideas and easy ways in which to incorporate this most important principle into your daily lives and remember "Learn how to store, what to store, preparedness in times of plenty, will comfort in times of lean".

APPRECIATION

A heartfelt thanks goes out to my husband Lonnie, for all the time he took out of his busy schedule to help me with the research and dedication it took to compile and piece this most important book together and to Les Hooper, my production manager at DMT Publishing, for such patience he had with me in designing this book.

COMPILATION

This emergency preparation book is a compilation of many different resources and learning curves taught to me over many years. I've relied upon my own understanding of what emergency preparedness is all about and the vastness of resources available to us online through FEMA, The Red Cross, Civil Air Patrol, Extension Services, CERT (Community Emergency Response Team), The LDS Church and much, much more . I am excited to be able to share it with you.

Catching the Vision of Self-Reliance

WE live in a most exciting and challenging period in human history. As technology sweeps through every facet of our lives, changes are occurring so rapidly that it can be difficult for us to keep our lives in balance. To maintain some semblance of stability in our lives, it is essential that we plan for our future.

On a daily basis we witness widely fluctuating inflation; wars; interpersonal conflicts, national disasters; variances in weather conditions; innumerable forces of immorality, crime, and violence; attacks and pressures on the family and individuals; technological advances that make occupations obsolete; and so on. The need for preparation is abundantly clear and a great blessing of being prepared gives us freedom from fear.

The council of Provident Living - enjoying the present while providing for the future is the opposite of crisis management. We want to plan for the future, not end up in a crisis for not being prepared.

This book has some wonderful information and resources to help in many areas, such as acquiring and storing a reserve of food and supplies that will sustain life. Obtaining clothing and building a savings account on a sensible, well-planned basis that can serve well in times of emergency. Understanding communications and survival techniques in the event of a disaster,   Simple first-aid instruction and simple ideas to help in putting important documents together in one location that are easy to grab in the event you need to leave your home and where family members know where to find them. All of these important ideas are part of Self-reliance and we're hoping you catch the vision as we proceed forward.

If Disaster Strikes

- Remain calm and be patient

- Follow the advice of local emergency officials

- Listen to your radio or television for news and instructions

- If the disaster occurs near you, check for injuries within your family. Give first-aid and get help for seriously injured people.

- If the disaster occurs near your home while you are there, check for damage using a flashlight. Do not light matches or candles or turn on electrical switches. Check for fires, fire hazards and other household hazards. Sniff for gas leaks, starting at the water heater. If you smell gas or suspect a leak, turn off the main gas valve, open windows, and get everyone outside quickly.

- Shut off any other damaged utilities

- Confine or secure your pets

- Call your family contact-do not use the telephone again unless it is a life-threatening emergency.

- Check on your neighbors, especially those who are elderly or disabled.

Great Informational Websites

Red Cross - www.redcross.org

Centers for Disease Control & Prevention - www.bt.cdc.gov

U.S. Department of Energy www.energy.gov

U.S. Department of Health & Human Services - www.hhs.gov

Federal Emergency Management Agency - www.fema.gov

Environmental Protection Agency www.epa.gov/swercepp

Different Types of Disasters

- Earthquakes
- Fire (Home or wildfire)
- Flooding
- Hurricanes
- Tornados
- Tsunami's
- Volcano's
- Thunderstorms
- Winter Storms
- Terrorism
- Dam Failures
- Landslides
- Heat Waves
-

These will be discussed in the "Disaster-Specific Preparedness Corner"

A Family Emergency Plan Needs to be Established

Your family should have a plan for how to respond to an emergency. Take time regularly to discuss and practice for emergency situations with your family. Have fire, tornado, or earthquake drills so that children will all know how to safely exit your home and where to gather.

In planning for emergencies, consider what would happen if a parent or another family member were not at home during an emergency. Would the family members at home be able to respond to the emergency? Responsibilities for emergency response should be divided and often duplicated among family members so that regardless of who is at home, the family will still be able to respond properly. You should have a plan for how family members will contact one another if the family is scattered during the emergency. This may include having a prearranged meeting place, a code word, or a relative's phone number.

Knowledge of first aid procedures will be invaluable for your family during any type of emergency situation. Younger children can learn most of these procedures, even CPR. First aid classes are offered at many locations within most communities. The Red Cross chapter in your community generally will offer a good basic first aid course, several types of first aid handbooks including a wilderness and boating specific type handbooks, and even first aid kits for purchase or occasionally that you can assemble yourself. The Community Emergency Response Training (CERT) classes are very good for emergency preparation. Neighbors can participate in emergency training together to share their skills.

The best advice Lonnie & I can give you is:

TO JUST... START!

Start putting a family plan together now!

TABLE OF CONTENTS

Over 300 pages of Preparedness Information

Back to Basics Corner

Back to Basics Corner

Simple steps to help you in this corner:

1. Understand your basic needs

2. Get family together; discuss emergency needs

3. Make an emergency contact phone list for each family member

4. Prepare or purchase 72 hour kits for each family member

5. Prepare or purchase a disaster (tote) kit for your home

6. Prepare or purchase a emergency kit for your vehicles

7. Make or purchase a basic first-aid kit for home and vehicles

8. Learn your community emergency services and needs for disaster preparation

9. Practice and maintain your family emergency plan

10. Keep it simple, don't get overwhelmed, and have FUN!

Basic Preparedness

At the time of this writing, we are living in a recession, we've been though Y2K, 9/11, a mortgage crisis, bank failings, and worldwide terrorism at the highest peak we've known in our lifetime, what with the type of airborne toxins, EMP (electromagnetic pulse from a nuclear strike), anthrax fears, flu epidemics, global warming, on and on and on. If you're like me, you're concerned about the future, not only for yourself, but your spouse, children, grandchildren, pets, etc.

This book was prepared, researched and put into place to help you start a basic emergency program, that anyone could follow and learn preparedness strategies that are common in all types of disasters. You plan only once, make sure it's a part of your mind set and then you are able to apply your plan to all types of hazards. Being prepared can reduce fear, anxiety, and losses that accompany disasters. There are many things one can do to reduce the impact of disasters by preparing in advance, and, knowing how to be ready for the unknown, can bring comfort. In this corner (chapter) we will go over basic information & teach some basic preparedness techniques for the following areas:

* **Learn** how to get informed about hazards and emergencies in your area, that may affect you and your family members.
* **Learn** how to develop a family emergency plan
* **Learn** how to put together a 72 hour emergency kit for each family member
* **Learn** where to seek shelter from all types of hazards
* **Learn** how to identify the community warning systems and evacuation routes
* **Learn** what to do for specific hazards
* **Learn** basic First-Aid skills
* **Learn** contact information for Emergency Services
* **Practice** and maintain the family emergency plan
* **Learn** how to assemble a disaster supplies kit for home, vehicle, work, school - (this is detailed in the In Home/Vehicle Corner)

Back to Basics Corner

Basic Preparedness

Provided below is a list of recommended government and non-government sites prepared for us through the US Dept of Home Land Security that can help in broadening one's knowledge of disaster preparedness topics that will be presented throughout this book.

GOVERNMENT SITES	
Be Ready Campaign	www.ready.gov
Agency for Toxic Substances & Disease Registry	www.atsdr.cdc.gov
Centers for Disease Control & Prevention	www.cdc.gov
Citizen Corps	www.citizencorps.gov
Department of Commerce	www.doc.gov
Department of Education	www.ed.gov
Department of Energy	www.energy.gov
Department of Health & Human Services	www.hhs.gov/disasters
Department of Homeland Security	www.dhs.gov
Department of Interior	www.doi.gov
Department of Justice	www.justice.gov
Environmental Protection Agency	www.epa.gov
Federal Emergency Management Agency	www.fema.gov
Food & Drug Administration	www.fda.gov
National Oceanic & Atmospheric Administration	www.noaa.gov
National Weather Service	www.nws.noaa.gov
Nuclear Regulatory Commission	www.nrc.gov
The Critical Infrastructure Assurance Office	www.ciao.gov
The White House	www.whitehouse.gov/response
U.S. Department of Agriculture	www.usda.gov
U.S. Fire Administration	www.usfa.fema.gov
U.S. Fire Administration Kids Page	www.usfa.fema.gov/kids
U.S. Geological Survey	www.usgs.gov
U.S. Office of Personnel Management	www.opm.gov/emergency
U.S. Postal Service	www.usps.gov
USDA Forest Service Southern Research Station	www.wildfireprograms.com
NON-GOVERNMENT SITES	
American Red Cross	www.redcross.org
Institute for Business & Home Safety	www.ibhs.org
National Fire Protection Association	www.nfpa.org
National Mass Fatalities Institute	www.nmfi.org
National Safety Compliance	www.osha-safety-training.net
The Middle East Seismological Forum	www.meieisforum.net

Back to Basics Corner

Basic Preparedness

Getting Informed about Hazards in your Area

The Homeland Security Advisory System was set into place to provide a comprehensive means to disseminate information regarding the risk of terrorist acts and other threats to and/or against federal, state and local authorities and directly to the American people. This system provides us with warnings in the form of a set of graduated "Threat Conditions" that increase as the risk of the threat increases. There are five threat conditions, each identified by a description and corresponding color.

In this day and age, there is always a risk of a terrorist threat. Depending on the type of threat, we, as the public, are alerted by the appropriate level and condition through media resources.

GREEN: Low Condition (Low risk)
BLUE: Guarded Condition (General risk)
YELLOW: Elevated Condition (Significant risk)
ORANGE: High Condition (High risk)
RED: Severe Condition (Severe risk)

These important descriptions can help in our process of knowing what to prepare for, and for instance, if the level was RED, the pre-preparation stage has passed and panic has set in. You would avoid public places, follow official instructions about restrictions to normal activities, listen to radio and TV regularly for possible advisories or additional warnings, prepare to take protective actions such as shelter-in-place (discussed later) or evacuation if instructed to do so by public officials, and contact employer and school facilities if problem is directly related to your geographical area.

Let us now discuss how to pre-prepare ourselves and our families, so that our levels of stress can be greatly reduced by our willingness to prepare in advance for any disaster or emergency.

Back to Basics Corner

Basic Preparedness

Getting Informed about Hazards in your Area

The need to prepare is real. Disasters disrupt hundreds of thousands of lives every year. Each disaster has lasting effects, both to people and property. If a disaster occurs in your community, local government and disaster relief organizations will try to help, but you need to be ready as well. Local responders may not be able to reach you immediately, or they may need to focus their efforts elsewhere. You should know how to respond to severe weather or any disaster that could occur in your area. These can come by way of hurricanes, earthquakes, extreme cold or hot weather, flooding, or terrorism, etc.

You should also be ready to be self-sufficient for at least three days or 72 hours. This may also mean providing your own shelter, first aid, food, water, & sanitation. Remember New Orleans.....

Getting informed and learning about the hazards that may strike within your own community is important to do the research on. This book will help in specific areas that you and your family will need to develop and include in your Family plan on how to escape from your residence, communicate with one another during times of disaster, shut-off household utilities, insure against financial loss, acquire basic safety skills, address special needs such as disabilities, taking care of animals, and seeking shelter.

1. Learn about the hazards and or emergencies that may strike your community, the risks you face from those hazards, and your community's plans for warning and evacuation. Your local emergency management office or the Red Cross is a good place to obtain this information. Research it out and write it down.

Natural Hazards: _____

Technological Hazards: _____

Terrorism: _____

Back to Basics Corner

Basic Preparedness

Getting Informed about Hazards in your Area

Warning Systems and Signals across America are broadcasted through the Emergency Alert System (EAS) and can address the entire nation in a very short amount of time in case of a grave threat or national emergency. This will come over the television, radio, and all public media airwaves.

Also in place is the National Oceanic and Atmospheric Administration (NOAA) Weather Radio (NWR) which is a nationwide network of radio stations broadcasting continuous weather information directly from a nearby National Weather Service office to specially configured NOAA weather radio receivers. Determine if this network is available in your area. If so, consider purchasing a NOAA weather radio receiver.

Basic Preparedness
Develop a Family Emergency Plan

Begin this process by gathering all family members together and review what potential threats or concerns could happen in your geographical area. You should have already contacted your local organizations to find out what those threats are.

Discuss with family members what to do if family members are not home when a warning is issued (see Communication & Family Location Corner). Additionally, your family plan should address the following areas:

* Escape Routes
* Family Communications
* Utility Shut-off & Safeguarding Your Home
* Insurance & Vital Records
* Special Needs
* Caring For Animals
* Safety Skills

Escape Routes

Draw a floor plan of your home. This can be done on a sheet of blank paper for each floor. Mark two escape routes from each room. Make sure children understand the drawings. You could even post a copy of the drawing somewhere within the walls of your home to help remind your family members what was decided. If, for instance, there were a fire, where will you meet once your family has gotten out of the home?

Make sure all family members understand that you will meet at the next door neighbors home or out on the sidewalk by the mailbox in your front yard, or by the telephone pole up against your backyard fence. Wherever the place may be, make sure all understand and do a mock run a few times too, for small children to understand. Please see diagram on next page of an escape plan.

Back to Basics Corner

Basic Preparedness
Develop a Family Emergency Plan

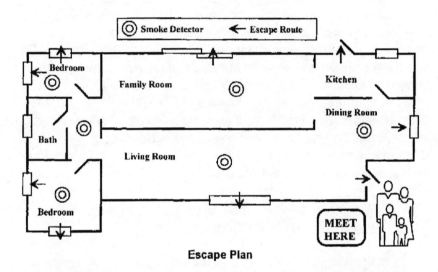

Escape Plan

Plan how your family will stay in contact if separated by disaster. A suggestion would be to pick two meeting places. One being a location a safe distance from your home in case of fire. The other would be a place outside your neighborhood in case you can't return home, and remember to choose an out-of-state friend or relative as a "check-in contact" for everyone to call. Post emergency phone numbers by every phone if possible. Install a smoke alarm and CO detector on each level of your home, especially near bedrooms; test them monthly & change the batteries twice each year.

Back to Basics Corner

Basic Preparedness
Develop a Family Emergency Plan

Family Communications:

Your family may not be at home when a disaster strikes, so plan how you will contact one another. Think about how you will communicate in different situations. Pick a relative or friend outside the state you live in to contact and let your family members know you are safe. This is very important, because if there is a crisis in your area, phone systems may be temporarily down. Make sure all family members have that contact phone number with them at all times. You can go to our communications corner (Communications and Family Location Corner) to find a detailed and lengthy list of different ideas to incorporate into your family plan.

Utility Shut-off & Safeguarding Your Home:

Learn how and teach family members where to shut off electrical power, gas and water to your home. Natural gas leaks and explosions are responsible for a significant number of fires following disasters. Because there are different gas shut-off procedures for different gas meter configurations, it is important to contact your local gas company for guidance on preparation and response regarding gas appliances and gas service to your home. If you smell gas or hear a blowing or hissing noise, open a window and get everyone out quickly. Turn off the gas, using the outside main valve if you can, and call the gas company from a neighbor's home. Please see a gas meter diagram on next page.

Electrical sparks have the potential of igniting natural gas if it is leaking. It is wise to teach all responsible household members where and how to shut off the electricity at the home junction box. Please see an electrical box display on next page.

WARNING: Always shut off all the individual circuits before shutting off the main circuit breaker and if you turn off the gas for any reason, a qualified professional must turn it back on. NEVER attempt to turn the gas back on yourself.

Back to Basics Corner

Basic Preparedness
Develop a Family Emergency Plan

Water quickly becomes a precious resource following many disasters, (see "Water Corner" for more information). It is vital that all household members learn how to shut off the water at the main water valve in your home. The reason for this is cracked lines may pollute the water supply to your house. It is wise to shut off your water until you hear from authorities that it is safe for drinking. Also, the effects of gravity may drain the water in your hot water heater and toilet tanks unless you trap it in your house by shutting off the main house valve (not the street valve in the cement box at the curb-this valve is extremely difficult to turn and requires a special tool). Please see diagram below.

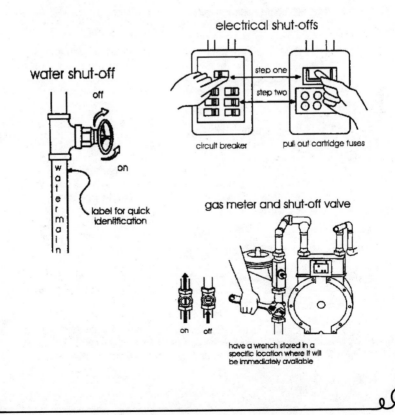

Back to Basics Corner

Basic Preparedness
Develop a Family Emergency Plan

Safeguarding your home is also a part of your plan.

Check for potential hazards:

1. Bolt or strap down top-heavy objects, such as bookshelves, china closets, water heaters and gas appliances, to prevent them from tipping over.

2. Place heavy and breakable objects on lower shelves, or in enclosed cabinets or drawers, such as canning jars, bottled goods, glass, vases, china.

3. Install and maintain smoke and carbon monoxide detectors throughout your home and natural or propane gas detectors near your furnace and hot water or boiler, and other gas appliances.

4. Keep properly rated and tagged fire extinguishers on hand and learn how to use them.

5. Store copies of important documents, such as insurance policies, deeds, property records, birth certificates, pass ports, trust paperwork, bank records of accounts, etc. in a safe place away from your home. Store originals in a fireproof/waterproof box or safe.

6. Keep matches, lighters, and flammable or poisonous products out of the reach of children and away from flammable materials.

7. Place flammable, explosive, toxic, and corrosive materials in lower or closed cabinets, preferably in garage, outside of the house, or in lower or closed cabinets or drawers and apart from each other.

8. Properly store and label flammable, combustible, explosive, corrosive, and hazardous materials.

9. Remove hazardous objects (i.e. mirrors, bookshelves, heavy pots, hanging plants, books, etc.) from above sleeping areas or move the bed.

10. Check electrical connections, gas pipes for faulty joints and connections, check to make sure home is soundly bolted or anchored firmly to its foundation and structurally safe.

Back to Basics Corner

 ## Basic Preparedness
Develop a Family Emergency Plan

Safeguarding your home is also a part of your plan by implementing preventive safety measures:

1. Know where, when and how to shut off the gas, propane, electricity, and water at the main switches and valves. Teach all responsible family members how and when to do this properly.

2. Learn basic First-Aid and CPR and put together a complete first aid kit and have every responsible person in your family learn how to use it.

3. Work on getting a 3 month, 6 month and up to a 1 year supply of food, water, sanitation, medical and fuel for your family.

4. Have a 72 hour kit made up for every family member.

5. Have a disaster supply kit made up for your home, vehicle, work, etc.

6. Keep a flashlight w/fresh batteries and/or a stick light in close proximity of sleeping quarters in every room.

7. Have an out-of-state contact telephone number that everyone can call to check-in with. It is usually easier during a disaster to call out-of-state than to call within the disaster area.

8. For your family emergency plans, work out a relocation plan detailing how you will get back together if you are separated during an emergency or disaster. Include a family evacuation plan from the residence, from the neighborhood, and/or the county, or state. Hold occasional drills, so that your family knows what to do during and after an emergency or disaster. Remember, if ye are prepared, ye shall not fear.

9. Have on hand a AM/FM radio with batteries crank or solar to keep in touch with the community at large.

10. Learn a new skill. Take a HAM radio class, get involved with CERT (Community Emergency Response Team), learn some basic scouting skills. such as, knot tying, camping, learning how to fish, learning weather patterns, backpacking, tracking, building a fire, etc. (The scouting motto is "Be Prepared")

Back to Basics Corner

72 Hour Kits

There is so much information out there regarding 72 hour kits. You can purchase them online through many different merchants, purchase directly from many store outlets such as Emergency Essentials in Utah or you can individualize one and put it together yourself. I will show you what is needed within this pack.

First off, the 72-hour or 3-day survival kit comes from military preparedness. Soldiers carried survival supplies, when involved in military operations to protect themselves, take care of their personal needs, and to complete their assigned mission. In other words, staying alive when forced into extremely dangerous or uncontrollable circumstances is what this survival kit is all about.

Having these kits ready for an unknown futuristic time will calm that helpless feeling caused by emergencies. Being prepared reduces the panic associated with the occurrence of uncontrollable future events.

Looking up the word "Preparedness" in the Wikipedia enclyclopedia, it states that preparedness refers to the state of being prepared for specific or unpredictable events or situations. Preparedness is an important quality in achieving goals and in avoiding and mitigating negative outcomes. It is a major phase of emergency management......

These kits can be designed and prepared for various purposes and places. For instance, your boat, your vehicles, work, college, and of course home, kits can be personalized to keep in all different locations.

72 Hour Kits

72 Hour Checklist ideas to personalize:

Food products - easy to use and eat
      MRE's - meals ready to eat
      MRE - heaters
      Candy/gum, chips, cookies - to calm children and nerves
      Jerky
      Canned meats, beans, potatoes
      Water - minimum 1 gallon per day
      Fruits - dried or canned (however canned will be heavy)
      Veggies - ready to eat
      Baby items - such as single formulas', food jars, powdered milk, etc.
      Energy foods - peanut butter, trail mix, etc
      Juices - boxed, canned, powdered
      Seasonings, sugar, salt and pepper, cinnamon, garlic or onion salt, etc
      Soups - bouillon, soup cups, ready-to-eat
      Energy food bars
      Water, water tablets, filters, individual packets

Utensils, tools and emergency items:

      Mess kit - individual or paper cups, plates & utensils
      Emergency Preparedness manual
      Batter-operated radio & extra batteries or solar polar
      Cash/coin
      Non-electric can opener
      Fire extinguisher, sm canister ABC type
      Tube Tent
      Pliers, wrench, hammer, screwdriver
      Tape, duct
      Compass
      Matches and/or birthday candles that don't go out when lit
      Aluminum foil
      Plastic storage containers
      Signal flare
      Paper, pencil
      Needles, thread
      Safety pins
      Whistle
      Knife or leatherman tool
      Lantern
      Flashlight w/extra batteries
      Rope, saw, shovel
      Playing cards
      Books & games

Back to Basics Corner

72 Hour Kits

72 Hour Checklist ideas to personalize, continued:

Sanitation:

> Soap, liquid detergent
> Feminine supplies
> Toilet paper, towelettes
> Personal hygiene items
> Plastic garbage bags, ties (for personal sanitation)
> Plastic bucket with tight lid or port-a-potty
> Disinfectant
> Household chlorine bleach

Infants:

> Diapers
> Outfits
> Wipes
> Food
> Formula
> Binky
> Blankets
> Bottles
> Infant tylenol
> Carrier
> Snacks
> Toys
> Utensils
> Sippy cup

Drugs:

> Personal drugs
> Aspirin or non-aspirin pain reliever
> Anti-diarrhea medication
> Antacid (for upset stomach)
> Syrup of Ipecac (use to induce vomiting if advised by the Poison Control Ctr)
> Laxative
> Activated charcoal

> _____
> _____
> _____
> _____
> _____

72 Hour Kits

72 Hour Checklist ideas to personalize, continued:

First-Aid Kit:

Sterile adhesive bandages in assorted sizes
Safety pins
Cleansing agent/soap
Latex glove (2 pair)
Sunscreen/chapstick
2-inch sterile gauze pads (4-6)
4-inch sterile gauze pads (4-6)
Triangular bandages (3)
Non-prescription drugs
2-inch sterile roller bandages (3 rolls)
3-inch sterile roller bandages (3 rolls)
Scissors
Tweezers
Thermometer
Needle
Moistened towelettes
Antiseptic spray/cream - Neosporin
Tongue blades (2)
Tube of petroleum jelly or other lubricant
Medicine dropper
Eye wash
Band-Aids
Rubbing alcohol
Insect repellant
Hydrogen peroxide

Clothing & bedding:

One change of clothing & footwear
Sturdy shoes or work boots
Rain gear, poncho, umbrella
Underwear, socks, t-shirts, including thermal underwear
Blankets or sleeping bag
Hat/gloves, sunglasses
Jacket, sweater
Emergency solar blanket
Heating pads/hand warmers to keep hands & feet warm

Animal Care:

Don't forget your pets in a crisis - make sure tags are up to date
Food, water, medications, pet carrier (if needed), etc.
Go to the Kiddie and Pet Safety Corner for more of this subject.

Back to Basics Corner

72 Hour Kits

A few years ago, I made 72 hour Kis for my grandchildren for Christmas. It was a lot less expensive to prepare my own, especially when you have as many grandchildren as I do (25 at count). This is what I included. These are only suggestions to help you start your own packs. Everyone has different tastes, and depending on the age of the person for whom you are making the pack determines what type of food items you will use.

A minimum of 4 liters of Water per kit is suggested.

Day 1
Breakfast – Granola, Hot Chocolate
Lunch – Macaroni & Cheese, ½ of Jerky & Juice Drink
Dinner – Ramen Soup, Crackers
Snack – Gum

Day 2
Breakfast – Raisins, Oatmeal
Lunch – Macaroni & Cheese, ½ of Jerky
Dinner – Peanut Butter/Jelly, Crackers
Snack – 1 Candy

Day 3
Breakfast – Granola, Apple Cider
Lunch – Trail Mix, Beef Broth, Fruit Snack
Dinner – Macaroni & Cheese, Raisins
Snack – 2 Candy

Recommended Rotate Date

_____

I purchased basic red, black and pink back packs from a store (Smith & Edwards), in Northern Utah. Whatever color you like is fine. However, red is a good emergency color, but when you have several kids in one family, I had to do color coding. I purchased the kind of backpack that has 2 pouches on the sides to put (2) bottles of water in for each child.

Now, for what I put into the pack is noted down below and buying the product in bulk made it a lot cheaper than going out and purchasing (1) at a time. The things that I added coincide with the 3 day menu plan noted on the left of this page. This was fun and helpful for my family at the same time. The products I put into these packs can be changed to fit your own individual needs. One more comment, (all food items were then put into a zip lock baggie with a copy of this menu). **HAVE FUN!**

1. (3) Mac-N-Cheese (instant)
2. 1 Top Ramen Noodles
3. 1 Peperoni stick
4. 1 Beek jerky
5. (2) Cracker snacks
6. 1 Trail mix
6. 1 Fruit snack
7. (2) Granola bars
8. 1 Oatmeal packet (instant)
9. 1 Rice krispies treat
10. 1 Peanut butter tube (ind. packet)
11. (2) Jelly packets
12. 1 Box raisins
13. 1 Capri Sun Drink
14. 1 Beef broth (instant packet)
15. (2) Bottles water
16. 1 Apple spiced cider (instant packet)

14. 1 Swiss Miss Chocolate (instant packet)
15. 1 Chicklets gum pack
16. (3) Cream savers (hard candy)
17. Toothbrush & toothpaste (individual size)
18. Matches (1 pack)
19. Whistle, compass
20. Soap, (small Individual size)
21. Kleenex (individual packet)
22. Lite Sticks (2) ea.
23. Mini First-Aid Kit
24. Mini Shampoo & Conditioner (saved from traveling, I had a bunch)
25. Emergency poncho
26. Solar blanket
27. Hand warmers (1) packet
28. Crayons, small pad of paper
29. Small packet of books (bought at $ store)

Back to Basics Corner

72 Hour Kits

More suggested 72 hr. menu ideas

Breakfast:
Pop tarts
Granola Bars
Cereal Bars
Instant Oatmeal
Fruit cup
Banana chips
Apple rings
Trail Mix
Carnation Instant breakfast drink
Powdered milk packet
Libby juicy juice box
Milk, aseptic box

Lunch & Dinner:

MRE's (meals ready to eat) plus a heater
Nalley's beef stew - sm container
Peaches snack cup
Pears snack cup
Tuna & cracker individual packages (yum)
Pudding snack cup
Peanut butter crackers
Lasagna - top shelf
Cup-a-soup
Cup-of-noodles
Sunflower seeds
Peanuts, planters individual packets
Hard candy - all types
Cream of wheat, instant individual packets
Beef jerky - all different types, individual packets
Applesauce snack cup
Fruit roll-ups
Cheese & pretzels
Cheese & crackers
Tea, coffee
Crystal light, tang
THE LIST GOES ON AND ON AND ON....

Membership clubs are great for these individual packaged food items bought in bulk.
REMEMBER, they need to be changed out 6 months to a year, depending on the
individual product. Pick a date and stick to it to keep this most important pack up to date.
What a small comfort this can be to have your emergency packs ready to go at all times.

Back to Basics Corner

Assemble a Disaster Supplies Kit

Home	Work	Car
your disaster supplies kit should contain essential food, water and supplies for at least three days. Keep this kit in a designated place & have it ready in case you have to leave your home quickly. Make sure all family members know where the kit is kept. Additionally, you may want to consider having supplies for sheltering for up to two weeks.	This kit should be in one container, & ready to "grab & go" in case you are evacuated from your work place. Make sure you have food & water in the kit. Also, be sure to have comfortable walking shoes at your workplace in case an evacuation requires walking long distances.	In case you are stranded, keep a kit of emergency supplies in your car. This kit should contain food, water, first aid supplies, flares, jumper cables, and seasonal supplies, such as blankets in the wintertime.

Since you don't know where you will be when an emergency occurs, prepare supplies for home, work & vehicles.

Back to Basics Corner

Assemble a Disaster Supplies Kit

WATER:
How Much Water do I need?

You should store at least one gallon of water per person per day. A normally active person needs at least one-half gallon of water daily just for drinking

Additionally, in determining adequate quantities, take the following into account:

> Individual needs very, depending on age, physical
> condition, activity, diet, and climate.
> Children, nursing mothers, and ill people need more water.
> Very hot temperatures can double the amount of water needed.
> A medical emergency might require additional water.

How Should I Store Water?

To prepare safest and most reliable emergency supply of water, it is recommended you purchase commercially bottled water. Keep bottled water in its original container and do not open it until you need to use it. Observe the expiration or "use by" date.

If you are preparing your own containers of water:

It is recommended you purchase food-grade water storage containers from surplus or camping supplies stores to use for water storage. Before filling with water, thoroughly clean the containers with dishwashing soap and water, and rinse completely so there is no residual soap. Follow directions below on filling the container with water.

If you choose to use your own storage containers, choose two-liter plastic soft drink bottles, not plastic jugs or cardboard containers that have had milk or fruit juice in them. Milk protein and fruit sugars cannot be adequately removed from these containers and provide an environment for bacterial growth when water is stored in them. Cardboard containers also leak easily and are not designed for long-term storage of liquids.

If storing water in plastic soda bottles, follow these steps:

Sanitize the bottles by adding a solution of 1 teaspoon of non-scented

Assemble a Disaster Supplies Kit

liquid household chlorine bleach to a quart of water. Swish the sanitizing solution in the bottle so that it touches all surfaces. After sanitizing the bottle, thoroughly rinse out the sanitizing solution with clean water. Fill the bottle to the to with regular tap water. If the tap water has been commercially treated from a water utility with chlorine, you do not need to add anything. If the water you are using comes from a well or water source that is not treated with chlorine, add two drops of non-scented liquid household chlorine bleach to the water.

Tightly close the container using the original cap. Be careful not to contaminate the cap by touching the inside of it with your finger. Place a date on the outside of the container so that you know when you filled it. Store in a cool, dark place. Replace the water every six months if not using commercially bottled water.

FOOD

The following are things to consider when putting together your food supplies:

> Avoid foods that will make you thirsty. Choose salt-free crackers, whole grain cereals, and canned foods with high liquid content.

> Stock canned foods, dry mixes, and other staples that do not require refrigeration, cooking, water, or special preparation. You may already have many of these on hand. Don't forget the manual can opener.

> Include special dietary needs as well.

Basic Disaster Supplies Kit

The following items are recommended for inclusion in your basic disaster supplies kit and we've included a check list over the next few pages to help you determine what to include in your own disaster kit.

Three-day supply of non-perishable food.

Three-day supply of water - one gallon of water per person, per day.

Portable, battery-powered radio or television & extra batteries

Flashlight and extra batteries

Whistle

Cash & coins

Photocopies of credit and identification cards

First aid kit and manual

Matches and waterproof container

Sanitation and hygiene items (moist towelettes & toilet paper)

Extra clothing

Kitchen accessories and cooking utensils, including a can opener

Special needs items, such as prescription medications, eye glasses, contact lens solutions, and hearing aid batteries

Items for infants, such as formula, diapers, bottles, and pacifiers

Other items to meet your unique family needs

If you live in a cold climate, you must think about warmth. It is possible that you will not have heat. Think about your clothing and bedding supplies. Be sure to include one complete change of clothing and shoes per person, including:

Jacket   Long pants

Basic Disaster Supplies Kit

Long sleeve shirt	Sturdy shoes
Hat, glove, scarf	Sleeping bag or warm blanket

Be sure to account for growing children and other family changes. See also a detailed checklist of disaster supplies. You may want to add some of the items listed to your basic disaster supplies kit depending on the specific needs of your family.

Maintaining Your Disaster Supplies Kit

Just as important as putting your supplies together is maintaining them so they are safe to use when needed. Here are some tips to keep your supplies ready and in good condition.

Keep canned foods in a dry place where the temperature is cool

Store boxed food in tightly closed plastic or metal containers to protect from pests and to extend its shelf life

Throw out any canned goods that become swollen, dented, or corroded

Use foods before they go bad, and replace them with fresh supplies

Place new items at the back of the storage area and older ones in the front

Change stored food and water supplies as needed. Be sure to write the date you store it on all containers

Re-think your needs every year and update your kit as your family needs change

Keep items in airtight plastic bags and put your entire disaster supplies kit in one or two easy-to-carry containers, such as an unused trash can, camping backpack, duffel bag or medium size tote.

Back to Basics Corner

Basic Disaster Supplies Checklist

Here is a checklist for your own individual kit.

Equipment & Tools

Tools	(√)	Kitchen Items	(√)
Portable, battery-powered radio or television & extra batteries		Manual can opener	
NOAA Weather Radio, if appropriate for your area		Mess kits or paper cups, plates, & plastic utensils	
Flashlight & extra batteries		All-purpose knife	
Signal flares		Household liquid bleach to treat drinking water	
Matches in a waterproof container, waterproof matches &/or birthday candles that don't blow out		Seasonings such as sugar, salt & pepper, cinnamon, garlic salt or powder, onion salt or powder, & other seasonings you family likes	
Shut-off wrench, pliers, shovel, & other tools		Aluminum foil, plastic wrap, zip lock baggies	
Duct tape & scissors		Small cooking stove & a can of cooking fuel, Dutch ovens	
Plastic sheeting		Comfort Items	
Tube Tent,		Games	
Compass, whistle		Cards	
Work Glove, knee pads		Books	
Paper, pens, & pencils		Toys for kids	
Needles & thread or small sewing kit		Hard candy, fun foods	

Back to Basics Corner

Basic Disaster Supplies Checklist

Here is a checklist for your own individual First Aid kit.

FIRST AID SUPPLIES

Supplies	Home (√)	Vehicle (√)	Work (√)

Back to Basics Corner

Basic Disaster Supplies Checklist

Here is a checklist for your own individual kit.

FOOD & WATER

Supplies	Home (√)	Vehicle (√)	Work (√)
Water			
Ready-to-eat meats, fruits, & veggies			
Canned or boxed juices, milk, & soup			
High-energy foods such as peanut butter, jelly, granola bars, trail mix			
Vitamins			
Special foods for infants or persons on special diets			
Cookies, hard candy			
Instant coffee, tea, crystal light			
Cereals			
Powdered milk, regular & chocolate			

Back to Basics Corner

Basic Disaster Supplies Checklist

Here is a checklist for your own individual kit.

CLOTHING, HYGIENE & BEDDING SUPPLIES

Supplies	Home (√)	Vehicle (√)	Work (√)
Complete change of clothes for each person			
Sturdy shoes or boots			
Rain Gear			
Hat, gloves, hand warmers, etc.			
Extra socks			
Extra underwear (thermal also)			
Blankets, sleeping bag & pillow			
Washcloth & towel			
Toothpaste & toothbrush			
Shampoo, comb & brush, mirror			
Deodorants, sunscreen, chap stick			
Razor, shaving cream			
Contact Lens Solution, extra eye glasses/contact lens			
Feminine supplies			

Basic Disaster Supplies Checklist

Here is a checklist for your own individual kit.

SANITATION SUPPLIES

Supplies	Home (√)	Vehicle (√)	Work (√)
Heavy-duty plastic garbage bags & ties for personal sanitation uses			
Toilet paper & towelettes			
Medium-sized plastic bucket with tight lid			
Disinfectant & household chlorine bleach			
A small shovel for digging a latrine			
Port-a-potty			

Back to Basics Corner

Basic Disaster Supplies Checklist

Here is a checklist for your own individual kit & these items should be placed in a watertight container for protection.

DOCUMENTS & KEYS

Item	Stored (√)
Personal identification	
Cash & coins	
Credit cards	
Extra set of house keys & car keys	
Copies of the following:	
➢ Birth certificate	
➢ Marriage certificate	
➢ Driver's license	
➢ Social Security cards	
➢ Passports	
➢ Wills	
➢ Deeds (Mortgage, Warranty, title)	
➢ Inventory of household items	
➢ Insurance papers	
➢ Immunization records	
➢ Bank & credit card account information	
➢ Stocks & bonds	
Emergency contact list & phone numbers	
Map of the area & phone numbers of places you could go	

Back to Basics Corner

Basic Disaster Supplies Checklist

Here is a checklist for your own individual kit.

SPECIAL ITEMS

For Baby	Special Needs For Adults	Home (√)	Vehicle (√)	Work (√)
Formula	Heart/Blood Pressure Meds			
Diapers	Insulin			
Bottles/Nipples	Denture needs			
Clothing	Contact Lenses & supplies			
Medications	Medications			

Back to Basics Corner

Seeking Shelter From Hazards

Taking Shelter is critical in times of disaster. Sheltering is appropriate when conditions require that you seek protection in your home, place of employment, or other location when disaster strikes. Sheltering outside the hazard area would include staying with friends and relatives, seeking commercial lodging, or staying in a mass care facility operated by disaster relief groups in conjunction with local authorities.

For effective shelter (see Outdoor Survival Corner), you must first consider the hazard and then choose a place in your home or other building that is safe for that hazard. For example, for a tornado, a room should be selected that is in a basement or an interior room on the lowest level away from corner, window, doors and outside walls.

Because the safest locations to seek shelter vary with each hazard, sheltering is discussed in the "Outdoor Survival and Disaster-Specific Corners" These specific chapters go into more depth and give recommendations for specific hazards on what to do and the different types of protection needed.

Even though mass care shelters often provide water, food, medicine, and basic sanitary facilities, you should plan to take your disaster supplies kit with you so you will have the supplies needed for your individual needs. Mass care sheltering can involve living with many people in a confined space, which can be difficult and unpleasant. To avoid conflicts in this stressful situation, it is important to cooperate with shelter managers and others assisting them. Keep in mind that alcoholic beverages and weapons are forbidden in emergency shelters, smoking is restricted and pets are not welcome.

The length of time you are required to stay in a shelter may be short,

Back to Basics Corner

Seeking Shelter From Hazards

such as during a tornado warning, or long, such as during a winter storm. It is important that you stay in shelter until local authorities say it is safe to leave. Additionally, you should take turns listening to radio broadcasts and maintain a 24-hour safety watch.

During extended periods of sheltering, you will need to manage water and food supplies to ensure you and your family have the required supplies and quantities. If you have not prepared yourselves, you are at the mercy of the sheltering facilities and will be allotted what is available at that particular time. These topics, water and food, will be discussed within the particular Corners "Food Storage Corner" and "Water Storage Corner".

Back to Basics Corner

Identify Community Warning Systems

Research needs to be done on your part once you've found out what types of hazards or disasters are likely within your area, to ask local officials the following questions about your community's disaster emergency plans.

Does my community have a plan?   yes ☐   no ☐

Can I obtain a copy?   ☐ yes   ☐ no

What does the plan contain?   _____

_____

_____

How often is it updated?   _____

_____

What should I know about the plan?   _____

_____

_____

What hazards does it cover?   _____

_____

_____

Identify Community Warning Systems

What about school emergency plans?

Know your children's school emergency plan:

> ➢ Ask how the school will communicate with families during a crisis

> ➢ Ask if the school stores adequate food, water and other basic supplies

> ➢ Find out if the school is prepared to shelter-in-place if need be, and where they plan to go if they must get away.

In cases where a school installs procedures for shelter-in-place, you may not be permitted to drive to the school to pick up your children. Even if you go to the school, the doors will likely be locked to keep your children safe. Monitor local media outlets for announcements about changes in school openings and closings, and follow the directions of local emergency officials.

For more information on developing emergency preparedness plans for schools, please log on the U.S. Department of Education at www.ed.gov/emergencyplan.

What about workplace plans?

If you are an employer, make sure your workplace has a building evacuation plan that is regularly practiced.

> ➢ Take a critical look at your heating, ventilation and air conditioning system to determine if it is secure or if it could feasibly be upgraded to better filter potential contaminants, and be sure you know how to turn it off if you need to

> ➢ Think about what to do if your employees can't go home

> ➢ Make sure you have appropriate supplies on hand

Back to Basics Corner

SPECIFIC HAZARDS

When it comes to a specific hazard, there are so many different types of natural hazards that could happen, and each type has a different action that should be taken before, during, and after an event, that time needs to be spent to cover this important topic. Information about the Specific Natural Hazards and what to do for each is provided in our "Disaster-Specific Preparedness Corner (Chapter)". Some on these hazards include:

➢ Flooding
➢ Tornados
➢ Hurricanes
➢ Earthquakes
➢ Extremes of winter cold & summer heat
➢ Different types of storms

Back to Basics Corner

Basic First Aid Skills

We all know how to use band-aids, but how much more do you know, if these skills were needed?

Can you perform CPR to save a life if needed?

Can you control bleeding?

Can you recognize and treat shock?

A small, but very important part of your first aid kit, is a booklet to help you through many items that you may not know or have forgotten. All these items and more will be discussed in our "First Aid Corner", and everyone should take a first aid class to learn what to do in an emergency. What if we were in a disaster crisis and there was no one to contact and you were left on your own?

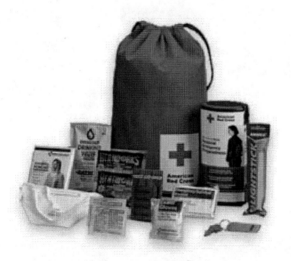

Back to Basics Corner

Emergency Phone Numbers

Main emergency number: 911 or _____ (local emergency number)

Fire Department local number: _____

Police Department local number: _____

Poison control: (800) 222-1222

Doctor: Name_____ Phone # _____

Hospital: Name_____ Phone # _____

Dentist: Name_____ Phone # _____

Local police: _____

Information About Child

First name: _____ Last name: _____

Date of birth: _____

Weight: _____ as of (date) _____

Medical conditions: _____

Allergies: _____

Health insurance: _____ Policy/group #: _____

Parent' Full Names:

Mom: _____

Dad: _____

Parent's Place ow Work and Phone Numbers:

Mom: _____

Dad: _____

Close Relative, friend or neighbor's name and phone number information:

_____

Practice and Maintain A Plan

Once you have developed your plan, you need to practice and maintain it. For example, ask questions to make sure your family remember meeting places, phone numbers and safety rules. Conduct drills such as drop, cover, and hold on for earthquakes. Test fire alarms. Replace and update disaster kits and 72 hour kits routinely.

One way we check our 72 hour kits is to have an annual picnic and all family members bring their 72 hour kits and eat from them. Then we replenish the product for another year for each individual kit. This can be fun and enjoyable gathering to go over many of the details and important information on your family emergency plan. Also, if something is not liked within a certain kit, it can be updated with something else at that time. This is a practice run through so things are ready in an emergency.

Pam & Lonnie Crockett at the Weber County Fair "Sheriff and Citizen Corps (CERT) Booth in 2008

Note: Much of the information contained in this Corner was taken directly out of and quoted from the FEMA "Guide to Citizenship Preparedness Manual" and the fema.gov website.

In Home/Vehicle Preparation Corner

In Home/Vehicle Preparation Corner

Simple steps to help you in this corner:

1. Make a household preparedness notebook/binder for all important documents and locate in one place

2. Organize important paperwork and know your account numbers. i.e. bank info, investments, insurance, etc.

3. Keep original records and important papers in a safe, secure location away from the house, i.e. safe deposit box; make extra copy for household notebook or other family members

4. Have a small amount of cash on hand for emergency purposes

5. Maintain an important telephone contact list; which includes numbers in and out of area

6. Prepare a basic safety supply kit/disaster kit and keep in a convenient place in your home & vehicle

7. A fire safety plan is important for the whole family and practice makes perfect

8. Keep your vehicles in good running order

9. Get in the habit of filling your vehicle fuel tank when the needle goes below the ½ full mark. (Find out why in this corner)

10. Keep it simple, don't get overwhelmed and have FUN!

Important Documents

Equally important as having food, water, clothing, and some money stored for now and future needs, is the need to have a copy of the family's financial matters documented and located in one place for instant access.

Take time now to organize your family's important papers, records and documents - it may well be the 2nd best investment you can make in your family's total preparedness activities.

The ability to prove bank and investment account and safety deposit box ownership may be necessary after a natural disaster or other calamity destroys important records. Not only having proof of ownership of certain property and assets, but securing rights to the use of property and qualifying for your earned benefits is tantamount in planning.

Keep original records and important papers in a safe, secure location away from the house. Making sure that all other family members know where important papers are located. Planning ahead saves a lot of agony, worry, time, and money – especially when an emergency or other unpleasantness causes debility, disablement, or death in the family.

While keeping originals in a safe, secure place away from the home, also keep & provide copies for other family members with instructions on how to access these originals, especially if located in a safety deposit box.

Important Documents

Helpful Hints To Get Organized

1. Make up a **Household Preparedness Notebook,** keeping critical information in one, easily accessible volume.

2. Prepare a safe place to keep this **Notebook.** Use the top loading plastic sheet protectors, with index dividers to identify the categories. Keep it updated.

3. Supplies for the **Household Preparedness Notebook** are available in office supply stores. The cost for everything one needs should not exceed $10-20

   Review what's needed:
   - Loose-leaf notebook
   - Top-loading sheet protectors
   - Index dividers
   - Waterproof, portable container

Checklist of Important Papers:
   — Family documents – birth, adoption, marriage, and death certificate
   — Relatives to contact (local and out of area) addresses and phone numbers
   — Social Security cards and entitlements
   — Passports
   — Medical records (especially prescriptions and eyeglasses)
   — Immunization records
   — Driver License
   — Military records

Important Documents

— Academic certificates
— Tax returns (prior 3 years)
— Estate Plan/Wills/Medical Directives and Guardianship
  Statement for your minor children (see "Finances In Order
  Corner" for more info)
— Insurance policies/life and property
— Retirement accounts/bank accounts
  & safety deposit box access info.
— Contents of safety deposit boxes
— Property and household items inventory (videos/dvd's and
  photos) Estate (see "Finances In Order Corner" for more info)
  Plans should have an inventory of the
  estate's property listed
— Record of credit/debit cards
— Titles to autos, equipment and other
  property including real estate
— Contracts
— Stocks, bonds, certificates, and other
  financial instruments
— Additional important documents that
  are important to you such as genealogy
  records
— Stash of cash – bills in small denominations
  and silver coins

It is also wise to have on hand, enough cash to meet your needs for
at least 2 weeks, longer if possible. If there is a man-made or
natural disaster, banks may not be open for awhile. Bank buildings
are also vulnerable to disasters and banks may have their records
destroyed, lending to the advice of keeping your bank records safe.

In Home/Vehicle Preparation Corner

Important Documents

In some circles, it is advisable to also have in your possession and in a safe location, gold and silver coin to use for barter, paying for someone's safety and just to have a valuable asset that is desirable and acceptable the world over. Since gold is now hovering around $900/oz, it is more practical to keep most of your precious metals stash in silver coin. Not collectibles, but 1oz silver medallions, because it is easier to break down in smaller amounts. It is way too costly to purchase gold in smaller fractions of an ounce because there is a premium added to the cost per ounce.

In a national emergency, paper money is sometimes worthless, but gold and/or silver is always acceptable. Find a reputable coin dealer and start purchasing some precious metals. Collectibles are fine, but you will pay a premium for the collector value. You want the intrinsic value, not the esthetic value of the coin.

Silver comes in many different medallion styles and as long as it is stamped .999 fine, it will not matter if it is a silver "coin" or medallion with "XYZ" stamped on it, it will suffice. Gold, on the other hand, comes in one oz. bullion coins (and smaller sizes and weights) minted by many countries the world over. The So. African Krugerrand is an example and can be purchased with very little premium added to the cost. The US government also coins/mints one oz. (and smaller) coins that are .999 fine and have just a little more premium added to the cost. If you decide to invest in some precious metals, you should always take possession.

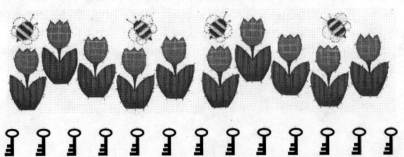

Important Documents

Remember, only keep copies in your home notebook. Keep originals in a safe, and secure location and inform family members as to that location and access details.

Waterproof all original documents and other items subject to water damage. Sprinklers might go off accidentally, even in a home. Flood waters might rise, even in a vault.

Fireproof all original documents as well. You can find fireproof safes at most places where safes are sold or repaired. Used fireproof safes can be found for 10% of the original cost and unless damaged, are as safe as new ones.

Remember to review and update your important documents periodically. How long should you keep those voluminous documents and records? The following table has some suggested guidelines as to how long certain documents should be kept.

Discard upon expiration or disposal of asset:

> Loan agreements (owed and owed to you)
> Bank account passbooks
> Lease agreements
> Auto Registrations/Titles

Short Term (1-3 years):

> Household bills
> Expired insurance policies

Important Documents

Medium Term (4-7 years):

Tax returns and supporting data *
Bank statements and account info.
Cancelled cks/ck registers (except for major purchases)
Paid loan documents

*Note: Federal and state tax laws change. Seek the advice of a professional tax preparer in your area for current requirements.

Long Term (permanent)

Marriage license
Adoption papers
Divorce documents/agreements
Checks and receipts for major purchases
Brokerage statements
Home purchase documents
Home improvement receipts
Business (self employment) records
Income property documents
Investment documents
Wills and Trusts/Estate Plan
Gift tax returns/records of gifts given
Inheritance documents
Medical records
Retirement records
Education records, transcripts etc
If self employed, By-laws and operating
agreements for Corps or LLC's

As part of your family's preparedness efforts, take the time NOW to organize your family's records. Recognize the importance

Important Documents

of being able to access your information while the federal, state, and local governments, financial, legal, and educational systems are functioning normally to assist you in your documentation. In any disaster of any magnitude, these agencies will not be there to assist you.

During any disaster or national emergency these agencies will be hard pressed to give any assistance and will not have the personnel to handle both the system failures and the requests for information overload. Though all of this may seem overwhelming at times, keep in mind: ***There is perfect order in the chaos of uncertainty.***

If you have minor children, and you have an Estate Plan with a Minors' Guardianship Statement, it is of primary importance to ensure that this is safe and that the appointed guardian also has a copy. In the event family members become separated, this will ensure your childrens' safety.

Personal disasters can be almost as problematic as a national or regional disaster. If a personal disaster occurs, such as an accident, or fire or death, surviving family members must have easy access to not only the important documents etc., but also know where to find important telephone numbers and how to call needed assistance. This is especially true if minor children are at home without adult supervision or cut off from other older/more mature family members.

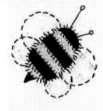

In Home/Vehicle Preparation Corner

Important Documents

Some suggested important telephone numbers are:

Nearest relative
Neighbor who would be willing to help
Ambulance or paramedic
Police/Sheriff
Family doctor
Pharmacy
Poison Control
Local Red Cross
Utility companies
Insurance Agent
Baby Sitter

Please see the "Back to Basics Corner" for more information on important telephone number lists.

Some planners suggest that each family keep what is called a **Disposition of Body** record so that the surviving family members will know if organs are to be donated, or if the deceased wishes to be buried or cremated.

Burial plots purchased in advance are also advisable and family members and friends told where the plots are located. After all, the price of real estate, including burial plots are continually rising in price.

Above all, during any disaster, whether it be personal, local, regional or national, all family members should be advised as to the whereabouts of all financial documents and given written permission to access them if the parents are not around.

Knowledge alone is not power, only the application of knowledge gives power to its owner.

Home Hazard Hunt

In any disaster, ordinary items in the home can cause injury and damage. Anything that can move, fall, break or cause a fire is a potential hazard. Go through your home and preview any of the following situations that could prevent problems in an emergency situation:

> Hang pictures or mirrors away from beds
> Brace overhead light fixtures
> Secure water heater, strap to wall, or use emergency kits for water heater stabilization
> Repair cracks in ceilings or foundations
> Clean & repair chimneys, flue pipes, vent connectors, and gas vents
> Weatherproof windows and doors in the event you have a winter emergency
> Fasten shelves securely
> Repair defective electrical wiring gas leaky gas connections
> Avoid overloading electrical outlets
> Flammable liquid hazards including gasoline, paint thinners, insecticides, oily polishing rags, should all be stored away from heat sources & stored separately in areas of open ventilation
> Learn where your shut-offs are located for electricity, water, natural gas, etc.
> Place large, heavy objects on lower shelves, including glass canning jars, books, small electrical appliances, etc.
> Have a family disaster plan in place
> Have a disaster kit ready at a moments notice (see "Back to Basics Corner")
> Have your families 72 hour (3-day)kits ready at a moments notice (see "Back to Basics Corner")

In case of Fire

It may surprise you that more people die in home fires than from all natural hazards combined. Frequently occurring between midnight and morning, fires are the disaster families are most likely to face. These fires are mostly unintentional, caused by poor wiring or careless behavior. Suffocation is the leading cause of death.

We talked a bit in the Back To Basics Corner about how to protect your home in case of a fire, but we will go into greater detail in this Corner. Below is a list of ideas to help protect your loved ones from fire.

> - Plan two escape routes out of each room.
> - Install smoke alarms and frequently check the batteries.
> - Teach family members to stay low to the ground when escaping from a fire.
> - Remember the phrase "stop, drop and roll" if clothing catches fire, this still applies.
> - Teach family members never to open doors that are hot. In a fire, feel the bottom of the door with the palm of your hand. If it is hot, do not open the door. Find another way out
> - Keep a whistle and a flashlight in each bedroom, to awaken household members in case of fire and for light after dark.
> - Check electrical outlets. Do not overload outlets
> - If you have a multistoried home, have a collapsible ladder for each upper floor level.
> - Make getting your family out a TOP priority and wait to call 911 when you are safely outside.
> - Consider installing home sprinklers
> - Purchase a fire extinguisher (A-B-C type) and teach family members how to use it. (See instructions on following page)
> - Close all doors behind you to cut off air movement to the fire, but don't lock them in case someone else needs to use them
> - If you are on an upper floor normally using an elevator, do not use that as an escape route, elevator shafts often act as chimney stacks for fires on lower floors.
> - Last but not least, remain calm, slowly head to the nearest planned exit and think through the consequences of all your actions

In case of Fire

Here is what a fire extinguisher looks like, the parts involved & a diagram on how to use this most important tool:

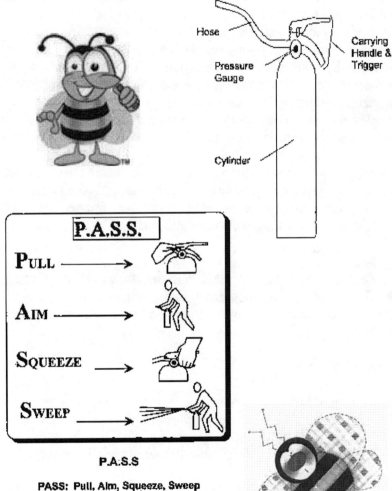

Hose

Pressure Gauge

Carrying Handle & Trigger

Cylinder

P.A.S.S.

PULL ⟶

AIM ⟶

SQUEEZE ⟶

SWEEP ⟶

P.A.S.S

PASS: Pull, Aim, Squeeze, Sweep

In Home/Vehicle Preparation Corner

In case of Fire

Have an escape plan in place:

In a fire or other emergency, you may need to evacuate your home, apartment or mobile home on a moment's notice. You should be ready to get out fast. Develop an escape plan by drawing a floor plan of your residence. Using black or blue pen, show the location of doors, windows, stairways, and large furniture. Indicate the location of emergency supplies (Disaster Supplies Kit), fire extinguishers, smoke detectors, collapsible ladders, first aid kits and utility shut off points. Next, use a colored pen to draw a broken line charting at least two escape routes from each room. Finally, mark a place outside of the home where household members should meet in case of fire.

Be sure to include important points outside such as garages, patios, stairways, elevators, driveways, and porches. If your home has more than two floors, use an additional sheet of paper. Practice emergency evacuation drills with all household members at least two times a year.

You can also find this information in the Back to Basics Corner in the front of this book. Just remember to practice your family escape plan, so you have no doubts as to how all your family members will know what to do.

Insurance Coverage:

Make a record of your personal property, for insurance purposes. Take photos or a video of the interior and exterior of your home. Include personal belongings in your inventory and keep this information with your Household Preparedness Notebook.

Make sure you have adequate home owners insurance, and other types of insurance you might want to check into are : Renter's insurance, flood insurance, earthquake insurance, vehicle insurance, health and life insurance.

Vehicles Ready

➤ Keep your vehicles in good running order.

➤ Keep your gas tanks full. On a yearly basis it doesn't cost any more to keep your tank full than it does to keep it empty.

➤ Keep containers of bottled water in your car.

➤ Keep some sort of snack (high energy food) in your vehicle at all times such as granola bars, raisins, peanut butter, crackers, etc.

➤ Prepare an emergency car kit that includes:
    flares
    flashlight with extra batteries
    jumper cables
    small fire extinguisher A-B-C type
    first aid kit with manual
    blankets (including space or solar)
    battery powered radio and extra batteries
    rain ponchos
    small pad of paper/pen or pencil
    hand sanitizer, small towels
    rubber gloves
    tire gauge
    small shovel
    pocket knife
    toilet paper (roll)

➤ Keep the tires at the correct pressure, using your tire gauge and it's also handy to keep a tire repair kit and pump in your car along with a spare tire.

➤ Keep a map of the area in glove compartment.

In Home/Vehicle Preparation Corner

Valuable Information

We've gone over the basic emergency kits such as the disaster home kit , the 72 hour or 3-day kit, both found in the Back to Basics Corner. We've discussed the emergency car kit in this **Corner** and the first aid kit in First Aid Corner. Some other kits that can be put together or purchased are known as the "Family Sanitation Kit" or "Porta-Potty Kit" which includes the following:

> 5-6 gallon bucket
> snap on toilet seat with lid
> chemical deodorant
> toilet paper rolls - as many as bucket will hold
> trash can liners
> additional items that can be added are:
>> vinyl gloves
>> nylon rope
>> clothes pins
>> laundry soap (small box)
>> gallon jug of water
>> hand sanitizer
>> bar soap
>> ready bath packets
>> porta shower
>> toothbrush & toothpaste

You can also put together an emergency "Personal Care Kit" which would include items such as:

> soap
> lotion
> hair brush, comb
> mirror
> wash clothes
> tooth brush, toothpaste, mouthwash, etc.

Valuable Information

Chapter overview checklist:

- ➢ Prepare a Household Preparedness Notebook
- ➢ Post emergency telephone numbers by phones
- ➢ Teach children how and when to call 911 or your local Emergency number
- ➢ Check if you have adequate insurance coverage on your home, personal property, health and life
- ➢ Teach each family member how to use the fire extinguisher (ABC type), and show them where it's kept
- ➢ Install smoke detectors on each level of your home, especially near bedrooms
- ➢ Conduct a home hazard hunt
- ➢ Stock up your emergency supplies including your disaster kit, 72 hour (3-day) kit, emergency car kit, etc.
- ➢ Determine the best escape routes from your home. Find two ways out of each room

Practice your emergency plan

- ➢ Quiz your kids every six months so they remember what to do
- ➢ Conduct fire and emergency evacuation drills
- ➢ Test and recharge your fire extinguisher(s) according to manufacturers instructions
- ➢ Test your smoke detectors every 6 months and change out the batteries at least once a year.

You will find some of the same information in this **Corner** repeated in other **Corners** because preparing for emergencies do overlap in their preparation.

Food Storage Corner

Food Storage Corner

Simple Steps to help you in this corner:

1. Take inventory of your present food storage
   (if none exists, that's O.K., you have to start somewhere)

2. Decide how you will purchase your supply
   (annually, monthly, weekly, by sales, etc.)

3. Decide which foods you wish to store
   (Basics, long term, short term, adding to basics, etc.)

4. Determine amounts of each product needed; use factor of:
   . (Male adult - 100%, Female Adult - 85%, Child - 50%)

5. Set some goals - this is a mind set

6. Stay on task, be consistent

7. Learn how to use your storage on a regular basis
   (Remember eat what you store and store what you eat!)

8. Organize your short term and long term pantries

9. Be sure to keep on hand a means of cooking
   (fuel, durable pots and pans, Dutch oven, B-B-Que, etc.)

10. Keep it simple, don't get overwhelmed and have FUN!

Food Storage Corner

From a bare cupboard

To a plentiful cupboad

Food Storage Corner

When you think of preparedness, one of the huge parts is your food storage. This can be an overwhelming task when thinking of the whole idea, but by taking the task and breaking it down into bite sized pieces, it really can simplify the larger goals.

Food Storage is a Mind Set

I will remind you of that as we proceed through this most important corner.

To start out, the following suggestions may be useful in helping to accomplish a food storage program for your family.

* Take inventory of your present food storage
* Decide which foods you wish to store
* Set some goals (see worksheets)
* Stay on task, be consistent
* Learn how to and use your storage on a regular bas
* Rotate and keep a continual inventory

I would like to teach you a plan that worked very well within our household and within our church community where we live. Keep in mind that turning this task into bite sized pieces will help simplify and accomplish the goal of storing food. All families are different in the way they eat, shop and cook foods. Most importantly and a motto of mine is, "Eat what you store and store what you eat." Keeping that in mind, depending on how you like to shop, here are different ways to incorporate this task into your family preparedness plan. We will show an annual, a monthly, and a weekly suggestion plan, any of which can suggest an easy course of action to take.

Food Storage Corner

Annual Food Storage Basics Plan

If you have the resources available to acquire your storage all at once, or buy it throughout the year, item by item until you have your years supply of food on the shelf, this plan can help. These are suggestions only.

These totals are per an adult male person at 100%. Use a factor of 85% for a female adult and a factor of 50% for a small child, to get the total amount needed for your food supply.
(For instance, when purchasing your supply of grains, if you have a male adult, a female adult & two small children in your family, you will have 400 lbs + 340 lbs. + 200 lbs. x 2 = 1140 lbs) :

350 - 400 lbs. whole grains, including wheat, rice, barley, millet, rye, buckwheat, pastas, flours, and specialty grains. You can combine all these or store just wheat.

Hand grinder for your grain storage, electric mills are great, but are a luxury item, not an emergency item.

60 lbs. sugar - including granulated white, brown, powdered, honey, molasses, corn syrup, jams, preserves, and specialty non-sugar mixes. You can combine all these or store just what you use.

8 lbs. salt - including seasoned salt, sea salt, kosher and basic salt

20 - 25 lbs. oils and fats - including cooking oils, olive oil, butters, including powdered, shortening, including powdered, salad dressings, and peanut butter. I would suggest combining all these, especially if you like peanut butter.

30 - 365 MRE's - These are instant ready to eat meals that can be left out on a rock during a sunny day and heated up, tear open and eat up. They're really tasty, but expensive. This is the easiest way to store your supply.

365 day supply of vitamins, vitamin "C", or sprouting seeds

18 - 20 lbs. powdered milk products - including regular, chocolate, and strawberry milk products and/or canned milks.

Food Storage Corner

Annual Food Storage Plan

14 gallons water - **minimum** emergency amount required for a 2 week period

60 lbs. legumes - including pinto beans, lima beans, lentils, split peas, kidney beans, soy beans, garbanzo beans, navy beans, great white northern beans.

2 #10 size cans - freeze dried fruits, such as apple or banana slices (very long term) or you can purchase cans by the case, including pears, peaches, fruit cocktail, etc.

2 #10 size cans - freeze dried vegetables (very long term) or you can purchase cans by the case, including corn, green beans, peas, carrots, beets, etc.

2 gallons vinegar - including white, apple or red

Seasonings, 1 container each of your individual tastes, including cinnamon, pepper, garlic salt and powder, onion salt and powder, chili powder, chicken bullion, beef bullion, vegetable bullion, oregano, curry, taco seasonings, all sorts of different pre-mixes for spaghetti, sloppy joe, gravies, on and on and

5 sm boxes baking soda

2 sm containers baking powder

1 lb. dry yeast for bread making, baking, etc

Condiments - your preference, including mayonnaise, mustards, ketchup, relish, B-B-Que sauces, bottled salad dressings, Worcester sauce, A-1 sauce,

Food Storage Corner

Annual Food Storage Plan

Beef Jerky - Several packets - your preference

Granola mixes, pudding mixes, - your preference

Drink mixes - tang, Kool-Aid, lemonade, tea, coffee, etc. (remember that you have to use water with these products)

Pop corn - your preference

Non Food Items - such as laundry detergent, bleach, dishwashing liquid, garbage bags, paper towels, toilet paper, tinfoil, plastic wrap, paper plates, plastic cups, plastic utensils, or individual mess or kitchen kits, etc.

Hygienic supplies - such as shampoo, hand soap, toothpaste, toothbrush, Q-tips, deodorant, brush, comb, razors, feminine hygiene etc.

First Aid supplies - First aid kit, band-aids, feminine and baby needs, antibacterial soap, antibacterial wipes, disinfectant, medications, aspirins, wound dressings, ipecac, hot/cold packs, burn free, insect repellent, sun block, eye protection, chap stick, on and on and on

Emergency supplies - hand crank radio, walkie-talkies, sewing kits, small amount of cash (bills and coin), port-a-potty, water purification tablets, privacy screen, whistle, flares, mirror, compass, folding shovel, sump pump, generator, rope, axe, saw, utility knife, gas shut-off tool, flashlight, candles, matches, trick happy candles that won't blow out to start a fire with, light sticks, batteries, stove, tent, sleeping bags, solar blankets, waterproof ponchos, ground cover, canned heat, hand warmers, extra clothing, emergency car kit and if I've missed something here, there is another list at the back of this chapter on other suggested items to include in your emergency storage plan.

Food Storage Corner

How to use the monthly planning system

Basic Item: Start here for planning your basic storage. If you already have the monthly listed item, check expiration dates, proper storage and amounts on hand. Replenish as needed. All of the categories of the monthly planning pages are suggestions only. The basic item's of the month can be changed for the needs of each individual or family. For instance, in January - we have water as our basic item, however, it can be changed to wheat, or beans. This system is to help as a guide to plan your own individualized food storage program and know where you will start and where you will finish. Figure out by month how much of each item you use and times it by 12.

Expanded #1 & #2 Items: Suggested items for those ready to move beyond the Basics.

Case Lot: - Suggested items to pick up from case lot sales and foods/non foods that are used frequently. Watch for sales and get these items as you can, not necessarily in the month suggested or as listed. Buy and stock up only on items you or your family like.

Home Canning: This suggested area will give you ideas on what you can do or learn

Non Food Item: These are usually a paper, hygiene or cleaning product to be purchased for storage

Tool Item: Something to use in your kitchen, home storage, or emergency kit.

Emergency Item: Items for 72 hour kits and household or vehicle items.

First Aid Item: Items for use in your home, vehicle, boat, cabin and also items to put together your own kits.

You can pick something in each category or work on just a couple categories.

Food Storage Corner

Month 1 or January
Monthly Storage Plan

Basic Item: Water - 14 gallons **minimum** requirement for 2 weeks per person, for instance if you have (4) people in your family, you will want to have at least 56 gallons of water stored

Expanded #1: Pancake mix, flour

Expanded #2: Scone & biscuit mix

Case Lot: Chocolate chips, hot cocoa mix, hard candies

Non-Food: Feminine needs, paper and pencils, color books, crayons

Tool: Solar flashlight

Emergency item: Hand warmers, waterproof matches, water containers

First-Aid item: Band aides (all sizes)

Items to add and make your own First-Aid kit: First-Aid manual and pick a container to carry first aid supplies in.

Food Storage Corner

Month 2 or February
Monthly Storage Plan

Basic Item: Oat Groats or oatmeal

Expanded #1: Granola, 6/9 grain mix, pearl barley

Expanded #2: Apple or banana slices in #10 cans

Case Lot: Ketchups, mustards, mayo, condiments, etc.

Home Canning: Canning jars and lids

Non Food: Paper plates, cups, utensils

Tool: Hand Crank Radio

Emergency Item: Backpacks (if making your
own 72 hour kits)

First-Aid Item: Sewing Kit

Item to add to kit: Plastic gloves, thermometer

Food Storage Corner

Month 3 or March
Monthly Storage Plan

Basic Item: Pasta (all kinds)

Expanded #1: Lasagna, shell, rotini,penne, acini di pepe,

Expanded #2: Flavor packets/mixes for spaghetti, tacos, gravy, sloppy joe, chili, etc.

Case Lot: Tomato soup, canned tomatoes, tomato paste, canned spaghetti sauces

Home Canning: Apple press, food processor

Non-Food Item: Dish soap, dishwasher detergent, Pine Sol cleaners

Tool Item: Hand can opener

Emergency Item: Make copies of all important documents and keep originals in a safety deposit box or fireproof home safe.

First-Aid item: Check and keep current on immunization records.

Items to add to Kit: Instant Ice Packs

Food Storage Corner

Month 4 or April
Monthly Storage Plan

Basic Item: Cornmeal

Expanded #1: Popcorn, corn flour

Expanded #2: Dried corn

Case lot: Canned corn, microwave popcorn, peanut butter

Home Canning: Seeds for planting a garden

 Non-Food Item: Baby and cleaning supplies

Tool Item: Hand Shake Popcorn Popper

Emergency item: Sanitation: water treatment and "port-a-potty", 5 gal. bucket/seat

Firs- Aid item: Antibacterial wipes, antibacterial soap, disinfectants

Items to add to kit: Diabetic supplies, baby supplies such as baby aspirin, ear bulb, etc.

Food Storage Corner

Month 5 or May
Monthly Storage Plan

Basic Item: Powdered Milk

Expanded #1: Nestle Quick chocolate or strawberry mix, Morning Moo, etc.

Expanded #2: Powdered eggs, powdered egg whites

Case Lot: Evaporated milk, sweetened condensed milk, baby formulas

Non Food Item: Tinfoil, plastic wrap

Tool Item: Hand egg beater

Emergency Item: Car kit, flashlight, flares

First Aid Item: First Aid Kit

Item to add to kit: Pepto Bismol (tablets or syrup), Tylenol

Food Storage Corner

Month 6 or June
Monthly Storage Plan

Basic Item: Oils and Shortenings

Expanded #1: Powdered shortening powdered cheese, powdered cottage cheese

Expanded #2: Pam spray, oil spritzer

Case Lot: Check for deals on dairy products, cheese's and butters (it is National Diary Month)

Home Canning: Canning salt, pectin

Non Food Item: Vitamins

Tool Item: Axe/hatchet, Duct tape

Emergency Item: Whistle, mirror, compass

First-Aid Item: Insect repellant, eye protection, sun block cream

Items to add to kit: Sterile gauze pads (all sizes)

Food Storage Corner

Month 7 or July
Monthly Storage Plan

Basic Item: Salt and peppers

Expanded #1: Baking soda, cornstarch, baking powder, baking cocoa

Expanded #2: Spices, bouillon, flavorings, extracts

Case Lot: Canned foods are usually on sale at this time, especially canned veggies.

Home Canning: *Zucchini relish - homemade

Non-Food Item: Paper towels, toilet paper, napkins,

Tool Item: Folding shovel

Emergency Item: Saw, utility knife, rope

First Aid Item: Aspirin, cough syrups, cold/flu medications such as Contac, etc.

Item to add to Kit: Scissors, waterproof tape

* use your own recipes or use the one at the end of this chapter

Food Storage Corner

Month 8 or August
Monthly Storage Plan

Basic Item: Rice

Expanded #1: Soup mixes

Expanded #2: Fruit drink mixes, pudding mixes, cake mixes, Jell-O mixes

Case Lot: Fruit for canning

Home Canning: Waterbath canning for fresh peaches, pears, tomatoes, *salsa, etc.

Non Food Item: Herbal supplements such as Echinacea, extracts, etc.

Tool Item: Gas shut-off tool

Emergency Item: Put together some small bills and coins for your 72 hour kits.

First Aid Item: Wound bandage dressing (all sizes), antibiotic creams or ointments

Item to put in kit: Same as items above

* use your own salsa recipe or use the one at the end of this chapter

Food Storage Corner

Month 9 or September
Monthly Storage Plan

Basic Item: Honey/Sugars

Expanded #1: Brown sugar, powdered sugar, Splenda

Expanded #2: Syrups, including Karo, maple, flavored

Case Lots: Vegetables

Home Canning: *Apple pie filling - homemade

Non Food Item: Laundry detergents, bleach, fabric softeners, stain removers, feminine napkins/tampons, diapers for children and elderly

Tool Item: Water spigot, pump

Emergency Item: Extra batteries, candles light sticks, lantern

First-Aid Item: A tool or item needed that is individualized to you or your family

Item to add to kit: Hygiene wipes

Food Storage Corner

Month 10 or October
Monthly Storage Plan

Basic Item: Wheat or other grain

Expanded #1: Cracked wheat, bulgur

Expanded #2: Yeast, gluten, dough enhancer

Case Lot: Soups

Home Canning: Dryer for fruits and veggie

Non Food Item: Toothpastes, toothbrushes, combs, razors, shampoos, hand soap, etc.

Tool Item: Wheat grinder (hand and electric) gamma lids, buckets, bucket openers, etc

Emergency Item: Camping stove, kerosene heaters, canned cooking fuel (Sterno)

First Aid Item: Q-tips, eyewash

Item to add to Kit: Eyewash, insect repellent

Food Storage Corner

Month 11 or November Monthly Storage Plan

Basic Item: Potatoes - purchase in 50# sacks

Expanded Item: Dehydrated pearls, flakes, slices, etc.

Expanded #2: Dried vegetables such as carrots, mushrooms, bell peppers dried onions, dried peas, etc.

Case Lot: Vinegars

Home Canning: Try drying fruit into fruit leather

Non Food Item: Garbage bags, small fire extinguisher

Tool Item: Basic tools, such as hammer, wrench, screw drivers, saw, pliers

Emergency Item: Bedding and shelter items, such as sleeping bags, wool blankets, solar blankets, tent, ground cover, etc.

First Aid Item: Safety pins, tweezers, cotton balls, heavy string

Item to add to Kit: Ace bandages

Food Storage Corner

Month 12 or December
Monthly Storage Plan

Basic Item: Legumes and nuts

Expanded #1: Split peas, lentils

Expanded #2: Sprouting seeds, canned peanuts, walnuts, almonds

Case Lot: Canned chili's, pork and beans, MRE's (meals ready to eat)

Home Canning: Learn how to make jerky using dryer

Non Food Item: Mess kits, paper plates, cups, plastic utensils, etc.

Tool Item: Seed sprouter

Emergency Item: Extra set of car keys, map of your area.

First Aid Item: Rubbing alcohol, prescription drugs.

Item to add to kit: Medicine dropper, splinting material, needles.

Food Storage Corner

Weekly Plan Instruction Ideas

Remember: Food Storage is a mind set.

It may take you a few years to get an adequate supply, but the key is to just BEGIN! and you'll be amazed at how quickly it all comes together.

1. Each week plan out what to search for and buy.
2. Get a marker for marking purchase dates, when you return home with your groceries/food storage.
3. Buy the largest amount you can sensibly afford; don't go into debt, but progress a little bit at a time.
4. Once you have purchased an item, learn to replace it, buy quantity. For instance, when I run out of Mayo, I start watching sales and when it's a decent price, I will buy several jars, not just one the way most people are used to shopping.
5. Watch for sales or other specials. This is the way to really stock up the pantry.
6. If you miss something, skip to the next week. Don't get overwhelmed. You will learn how to shop if you just start with something that is the easiest for you.
7. If something is not listed on the items that your family likes, don't hesitate to put it on the schedule.
8. Eat what you store and store what you eat.
9. Try to learn a new recipe each week, with storage items, you don't use as often, but that will stretch your budget.
10. If you will put forth the effort and try, you will be blessed for your actions.

Food Storage Corner

Weekly Storage Plan

(or) January

Week 1
Christmas items are usually 50% off. This is a great time to stock up for next year's holiday.

Week 2
Laundry & dish detergents, bleach, cleaners

Week 3
Medical Supplies: Aspirin, Tylenol, Pepto Bismol, Vicks, flu medicines, (whatever your family is used to needing for illness such as colds, flu, etc

Week 4
Paper Supplies: Paper towels, plates, cups, tissues, toilet paper, napkins, utensils

These are suggestions only, and on top of your weekly budget for groceries. However, if you can tighten up the belt and eat beans and soup for just one week a month, you can accomplish miracles. Watch the sales and instead of buying (1) item of bleach for instance, buy (6) and watch your storage grow....

Food Storage Corner

Weekly Storage Plan

(or) February

Week 1
Drink Items: Tang, Kool-Aid, Crystal Light, vegetable juice

Week 2
Peanut butter, butter, jams and jellies

Week 3
Solid vegetable shortening and or oils (vegetable, olive, corn, sesame, peanut)

Week 4
Personal hygiene products: soap, deodorant, shampoo, toothpaste, toothbrushes, etc

The dollar store is a terrific place to stock up on shampoo's toothpaste, toothbrushes, etc.

Food Storage Corner

Weekly Storage Plan

(or) March

Week 1
First-Aid Supplies: Q-tips, Band-aids, Neosporin, calamine lotion, hydrogen peroxide, etc.

Week 2
Mixes: Cake, pancake, muffin, Bisquick, cookie, etc.

Week 3
Spices & Herbs: Pepper, salt, cinnamon, oregano, garlic powder/salt, onion powder/salt, taco seasoning, chili powder, dried onions, etc.

Week 4
Rice: (long grain, brown, instant, risotto, etc.)

Week 5
Oat Groats or oatmeal, rolled oats, instant oatmeal, boxed cereals, etc.

The dollar stores are great for stocking up on your spices...

Food Storage Corner

Weekly Storage Plan

(or) April

Week 1
Beans: Navy, pinto, kidney, red, black, lima, soy, great northern, etc.

Week 2
Powdered milk products: Morning Moo, Hershey's (white, chocolate, strawberry)

Week 3
Pasta: Spaghetti, egg noodles, macaroni and cheese, (get what your family eats already)

Week 4
Garden seeds for planting your own garden, whether it is in pots or plots

Remember, you are buying for long term storage. For instance, buy a 25# sack of great northern beans, a 25# sack of kidney beans, 25# sack of pinto beans & a 25# sack of soy beans or you can buy a case of each to stock up your food storage. Watch the sales...

Food Storage Corner

Weekly Storage Plan

(or) May

Week 1
Grains: Hard wheat (white or red), rye, barley, flour

Week 2
Dry soups and soup mixes or canned soups

Week 3
Pudding mixes, Jell-O gelatin

Week 4
72 hour kits: Start it, update it, and complete it. Be sure to check clothing sizes in an update

Week 5
Vitamins, C, B-complex, calcium, etc.

Remember, this is an on going mind set. We are working on obtaining a nice food storage. Everyone eats and cooks differently, so items may be changed to your own personal needs. If you can stay with a plan, the outcome will be terrific!

Food Storage Corner

Weekly Storage Plan

(or) June

Week 1
Matches, Candles, extra batteries, good flashlight, canning jar lids (great bartering tool), compass

Week 2
Water week: Case lot, gallon jugs, fill up 2 liter bottles, prepare water bath and fill canning jars with water

Week 3
Condiments: Ketchup, mustards, relishes, mayo, etc.

Week 4
Sleeping bags, thermal blankets, tent, mattress (air or foam)

Even though you may not go camping, sleeping bags and a tent are emergency preparedness items in disasters or emergency situations.

Food Storage Corner

Weekly Storage Plan

(or) July

Week 1
Break time: Look to sales and buy something for your food or emergency storage

Week 2
Break time: Look to sales and buy something for your food or emergency storage

Week 3
Get caught up time: If you missed a week, use this one to catch up...

Week 4
Canned Goods: Chili's, canned meats, green beans, corn, carrots, beets, etc.

Grocery Stores around the country start their case lot sales in July and August. This is a perfect time to purchase canned goods at a great price! Remember quantity is the goal...

Food Storage Corner

Weekly Storage Plan

(or) August

Week 1

Back-to-School: Paper, pencils, crayons, envelopes, stamps, etc.
(for those of you that don't have children to buy for, use this week
as time to purchase your own paper/book supplies)

Week 2

Baking week: Baking powder, soda, cornstarch, yeast, bouillon
cubes, cooking spray, vanilla (Even if you don't bake, this is
for storage purposes and great for bartering. Also, learn to cook
from scratch. It tastes so much better than out of a box or can!)

Week 3

Tomato week: Salsa, juices, sauces, paste, whole/chopped
canned tomatoes, and pizza or spaghetti sauces

Week 4

Try canning this week: Canning jars, bulk fruit, bulk tomatoes,
or dehydrate some fruit or tomatoes.

Week 5

Long term: #10 size cans of fruit or veggies (freeze dried)

**Try a new skill like canning;
do the research and find out
how simple this can be. If you
don't want to try this, then use
this week to catch up on
something...**

Food Storage Corner

Weekly Storage Plan

(or) September
Week 1

Vegetable week: Canned, frozen or fresh green beans, corn, carrots, peas, mushrooms, onions (whatever the family likes)

Week 2

Potato week: Bulk storage potatoes, such as russets, reds, yukon golds, also try dried or canned, etc.

Week 3

Honey week: Watch the sales, if you have a honey distributor in your area, take your own canning jars and get them filled or purchase in cans or jugs.

Week 4

Work on your 72 hour kits: Add something, or maybe a solar radio for emergency preparedness

> **Winter is just around the corner, and it wasn't raining when Noah built the Ark. There isn't time to build lifeboats after the ship has sprung a leak or make a parachute when a plane goes into a spin, but if you're prepared ye shall not fear!**

Food Storage Corner

Weekly Storage Plan

(or) October

Week 1

A small shovel, hand can-opener, wind-up clock,
porta-potty, batteries

Week 2

Plastic bags: Freezer bags, plastic wrap
wax paper, garbage bags, aluminum foil,
plastic containers, etc.

Week 3

Apple Week: Make at least (1) item from apples,
pie filling, applesauce, juice, apple butter, dehydrate
apples cut into slices (your home will smell absolutely
wonderful!) I love apples, it reminds me of fall and hot
cider and cozy moments with my grandchildren...

Week 4

Vinegars: Red, wine, apple, white

Week 5

Long term storage such as: Powdered eggs, powdered
cheese, MRE's (meals ready to eat)

Food Storage Corner

Weekly Storage Plan

(or) November

Week 1

Sweet Week: Sugars, (white, brown, powdered), corn syrup, cocoa powder, chocolate chips, nuts, fun, fun, fun!

Week 2

Great week to shop the sales!

Week 3

Great week to shop the sales!

Week 4

Emergency Auto kit: Make one or purchase one, or update one

The holidays are coming upon us, family and friends gathering, makes it a hustle, bustle time, with no time to think much about anything else. Give yourself a break if you need to.

Food Storage Corner

Weekly Storage Plan

(or) December

Week 1

Popcorn - (purchase in 25# or 50# sacks for a lot less),
cider mixes, evaporated milk, sweetened condensed milk,
hot cocoa mixes, etc.

Week 2

Gravy packets, salad dressing mix packets, seasoning
packets, stuffing mixes, cranberry sauces, roll mixes, etc.

Week 3

Small First-Aid kit - (purchase, make, or update)

Week 4

Merry Christmas to all!!!

Week 5

Remember this is a mind set! Don't stop!
Nuts and hard candy (these should be 50% off after
Christmas)

> We are coming to the close
> of another year and looking
> forward. Where are you on
> your food storage plan? Don't
> stop, just go forward and you'll
> be blessed for it.

Food Storage Corner

Grocery List Ideas

The following pages will help with ideas on how to start
a food storage program. Everyone thinks differently and has
different needs. Some of you will have some sort of food storage
already in your pantry and some will be starting from the
beginning. Some of you have large families to buy for and some of
you will only have yourself. These lists will help give you ideas on
how to start your own lists. Remember, food storage is a mind set.
You need to start with the basics and move out from there.

Preparing your list, either weekly, monthly, or annually is going to
take some work, and as you go along, things will change, or
something may become more important than something already on
your list. Don't feel you have to stick right to a list, it should
always be evolving, until one day, you can have a nice food storage
to feel good about.

Food Storage Corner

Grocery List Ideas - Monthly

TO STOCK UP YOUR PANTRY

Basic Item:	RICE - 75#'s
Expanded Items:	TANG - DRINK MIX - 4 canisters
	_____
	_____
	_____
Case Lot Sale:	TOMATO SOUP - 24 cans/case
	VEGETABLE BROTH - 12 cans/case
	PORK & BEANS - 24 cans/case
Canning Items:	NOT THIS MONTH
	_____
	_____
Non-Food Items:	FOOD BUCKETS to store grains - 20
	GAMMA LIDS - 5
	_____
Tool:	BUCKET OPENER
Emergency Items:	CANDLES - pick up at dollar store
	LARGE BOX OF MATCHES
First Aid Items:	ALL SIZES OF BAND-AIDS

Food Storage Corner

Grocery List Ideas - Monthly

TO STOCK UP YOUR PANTRY

Basic Item:	SALT - 25#'s
Expanded Items:	BAKING SODA - 5 BOXES
	CORNSTARCH - 5 BOXES
	BAKING POWDER - 5 CANNISTERS
	YEAST CAKES - 10 PKGS
Case Lot Sale:	NOT THIS MONTH
Canning Items:	LARGE LIDS FOR CANNING JARS
	_____
	_____
Non-Food Items:	TOILET PAPER - 2 CASES
	PAPER TOWELS - 1 CASE
	_____
Tool:	FOLDING SHOVEL
Emergency Items:	WHISTLES FOR FAMILY 72 HR KITS
First Aid Items:	GET IMMUNIZATION RECORDS IN ORDER

Food Storage Corner

Monthly Grocery List

Basic Item: _____

Expanded Items: _____

_____

_____

Case Lot Sale: _____

_____

_____

Canning Items: _____

_____

_____

Non-Food Items: _____

_____

_____

Tool: _____

Emergency Items: _____

_____

First Aid Items: _____

Food Storage Corner

Weekly Grocery List Ideas

Work within your budget when making your lists

Week #1   BUCKETS TO STORE GRAINS (4)

                 GAMMA LID(S) - 2

                 _____

                 _____

Week #2   POP CORN - 25# SACK

                 PEANUT BUTTER - 5 EA.

                 STRAWBERRY JAM - 6 EA.

                 _____

Week #3   POWDERED EGGS - 1 #10 size can

                 SALT - 25# SACK

                 _____

                 _____

Week #4   FIRST AID KIT

                 BAND-AIDS

                 FLASHLIGHT FOR EACH BEDROOM

                 _____

Food Storage Corner

Weekly Grocery List Ideas

Work within your budget when making your lists

Week #1   SUGAR - 25# SACK

                     PINTO BEANS - 25# SACK

                     _____

                     _____

Week #2   POWDERED MILK - (2) #10 CANS

                     _____

                     _____

Week #3   PANCAKE SYRUP - 2 ea. 1 gal jugs

                     _____

                     _____

Week #4   BLEACH (on sale) 6 ea.

                     SHAMPOO (on sale) 6 ea.

                     _____

> Everybody shops differently. Make your list according to your needs, but remember, you are stocking up your pantry supply and emergency supplies in your home. If you can get into this mind set, you will be amazed at what you can accomplish.

Food Storage Corner

Weekly Grocery List

These Items are on top of your normal grocery items:

Week #1

_____

_____

_____

_____

Week #2

_____

_____

_____

_____

Week #3

_____

_____

_____

_____

Week #4

_____

_____

_____

_____

Food Storage Corner

Basic Storage Needs Per Adult Male

Use a factor of 85% for an adult female and a factor of 50% for a small child. For instance, when purchasing grains, if you have an adult male, an adult female and two small children in your family, you will use this formula:

400 lbs. + 340 lbs. + 200 lbs + 200 lbs = 1140 lbs.

Whole Grains - including wheat, rice, oats, barley, millet, rye, buckwheat, pastas, and specialty grains.

Per Adult Person -   350- 400 lbs.   x _____ = _____

Sugars - including granulated, brown, powdered, honey, molasses, corn syrup, jams or preserves & specialty non-sugars
                                    60 - 75 lbs   x _____ = _____

Salts - including seasoned salt, sea salt, and basic salt
                                    8 lbs.   x _____ = _____

Oils and fats - including cooking oils, olive oil, butters - including powdered, shortening - including powdered, salad dressings, and peanut butter
                                    20 - 25 lbs   x _____ = _____

Water - **minimum** emergency amount per person - 14 gallons for a 2 week period
                                    14 gal   x _____ = _____

Powdered Milk - including regular, chocolate, strawberry, and canned milk products
                                    18 - 20 lbs.   x _____ = _____

Legumes - including pinto beans, lima beans, lentils, split peas, kidney beans, soy beans, garbanzo beans, navy beans, great white northern beans.
                                    60 lbs.   x _____ = _____

Seasonings - including garlic salt and powder, onion salt and powder, cinnamon, pepper, chili powder, chicken bullion, beef bullion, baking soda (1lb), baking powder (1 lb.), dry yeast (depending on tastes, each individual is different in their needs)
                                                x _____ = _____

Food Storage Corner

Goals Worksheet

Decide whether you will work on your food storage:

Weekly _____

Monthly _____

Annually _____

Short Term Goals (Ideas- write them down):

72 hour kits for each person in the family _____

Food Storage Basics - (grains), 3 month supply _____

6 month supply _____

1 year supply _____

Hand Grinder/Mill _____

Water Storage - (2 week minimum supply) _____

Long Term Goals (ideas- write them down):

Food Storage Necessities (each family is different)

_____

Non Food Necessities (toilet paper, laundry soap, shampoo)

_____

Emergency Preparation (porta-potty, water purification tablets, sewing kits, hand crank radio, hand can opener)

_____

Food Storage Corner

Canning Recipes

Zucchini Relish

Yummy

5 lbs. medium size zucchini
6 large onions, coarsely chopped
½ cup salt
2 cups white wine vinegar
cold water
1 cup sugar
1 tsp. dry mustard
2 tsp. celery seed
½ tsp. each ground cinnamon, nutmeg, & pepper
1 sm jar chopped pimentos - for color

Place zucchini and onions in a food processor or force through a food chopper until finely chopped. Place in a bowl, sprinkle with salt, and cover with water. Cover and refrigerate at least 4 hours or until next day. Drain vegetables, rinse well, and then drain again. Place in a 5 or 6 qt. pot along with vinegar, sugar, mustard, celery seed, cinnamon, nutmeg, pepper, and pimentos. Bring to a boil over high heat, stirring occasionally. Reduce heat and simmer, uncovered and stirring occasionally, until reduced to about 3 qts. (about 20 min.) Meanwhile, prepare 6 pint-size canning jars, following steps for water bath procedure. Process for 15 minutes.
Makes 6 pints

Yummy

Canned Salsa

6 cups fresh or canned tomatoes
1 sm can tomato paste
1 sm onion, chopped
1 cup celery, chopped
1 cup green pepper, chopped

continued on next page

Food Storage Corner

Canning Recipes

1 4 oz can diced green chili's
1 tsp lemon juice
1 tsp garlic salt
1 tsp chili powder
1 tsp cumin
1 tsp salt
1/4 tsp red (cayenne) pepper (more or less - your preference)
1/4 cup sugar (more or less - your preference)

If using fresh tomatoes, drop tomatoes in boiling water for 1 minute, take out and drop into ice water (very easy to peel this way), squish or chop, add to pot with all other ingredients, stir and simmer all ingredients 1 to 1 ½ hrs. Place in cleaned canning jars and water bath for 20 minutes.

Apple Pie Filling

5 ½ - 6 lbs. apples
syrup:
4 ½ cups sugar
1 cup corn starch
2 tsp cinnamon
½ tsp nutmeg
1 tsp salt
3 T lemon juice
2-3 drops food coloring (yellow)

Yummy

Slice apples into water mixture that has either 1 T vinegar and 1 T salt or 1 T fresh fruit, or 1 T lemon juice to keep the apples from browning. On medium heat, add all syrup ingredients above, except lemon juice and food coloring. Cook until think and bubbly. Remove from heat and add lemon juice and food coloring. Pack apple slices into clean canning jars and pour syrup over apples up to ½ from top. Process in water bath for 20 minutes.

Makes approximately 6 quarts

Food Storage Corner

Other Suggested Items for Storage

Aluminum foil (heavy duty)
Ammonia
Aprons
Ascorbic acid
Axe,
Baby toys
Baby supplies (diapers, bottles, wipes, etc)
Bar soap and shampoo
Barbecue spatulas, grills, forks, tongs, etc
Batteries
Blankets and bedding
Bleach, liquid & powder
Borax
Bottle and can openers
Broom, carpet sweeper, dust pan, mop heads
Buckets with tight fitting lids
Camping equipment
Candles and candle holders
Canned hear (Sterno or alcohol)
Canning jars, rings and lids
Cast iron Dutch ovens, skillets and griddles
Chainsaw, splitters and wood saw
Charcoal briquettes and lighter fluid
Cheesecloth and burlap sacks
Combs and brushes
Construction tools (hammer, saw, level, etc.)
Cooking and eating utensils (mess kits)
Deodorants
Dish soap and dish cloths
Disinfectants and alcohol
Duct and masking tape
Extra eye glasses or contact cleaning solutions
Extra set of clothing and coats for everyone
Feminine hygiene needs - continued

Food Storage Corner

Other Suggested Items for Storage

Fire extinguishers (class ABC)
Firearms and ammunition
Firewood (at least 2 cords) or coal
Fishing and hunting supplies & equipment
First-aid kits and special medications
Flashlights and extra bulbs and/or light sticks
Fuel
Games for children and adults
Garbage bags and liners (plastic in sorted sizes)
Garbage cans with tight fitting lids
Garden hose for siphoning and fire control
Garden tools (rake, shovel, hoe, wheel barrow, sm tools)
Gas masks and/or dust masks
Generator - small and portable
Gloves and hats (both winter and work)
Hand pump and siphons
Household cleaning supplies
Ice chest
Insect repellants and traps
Kitty litter
Knee pads
Laundry detergent
Life jackets (for flood prone areas)
Lime (chlorinated)
Lumber
Lye
Latches and fire starters
Measuring spoons, cups and droppers
Mouse and rat traps and poison
MRE's (meals ready to eat)
Nails, screws, nuts and bolts
Newspapers for first aid splits and wrapping water material
Nursing needs
Paper plates
Paper for writing - continued

Food Storage Corner

Other Suggested Items for Storage

Pencils and pens
Pet food and supples
Plastic pails with tight lids or gamma seals
Plastic wrap, zip lock baggies all sizes, wax paper
Plastic sheeting (heavy duty)
Port-a-potty or bucket with tight fitting lid
Pots and pans - Dutch ovens
Potting soil and seed starting containers
Power cords and plugs
Propane or kerosene fuel
Push lawn mower and sickles
Radiation monitoring equipment (dosimeter)
Radio (am/fm battery and/or solar powered)
Rags/cloths
Rope, string, bailing wire and twine
Seed sprouting kit
Seeds for planting and fertilizer
Sewing needles, thread, notions and fabric
Shaving needs
Short wave CB or HAM radio
Sleeping bags, pillows, tents
Split wood or coal for heating
Sponges and scouring pads
Straight razor blades
Thermos jugs and coolers
Thyro-Block (potassium iodide) tablets
Toilet and facial tissue by the case
Toothpaste and toothbrushes and denture care
Towels and wash clothes
Walkie-talkies
Wash tubs or basins
Water filters and filtration units
Water purification tablets
Wheat grinder (hand or electric)
Wind-up alarm clock, watch

Food Storage Corner

SHOPPING LIST

_____

_____

_____

_____

_____

_____

_____

Water Storage Corner

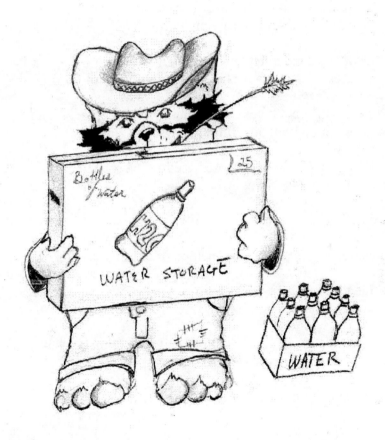

Water Storage Corner

Simple steps to help you in this corner:

1. A 3-day supply of drinking water per person is a must!

2. Decide how you will store your water
   (Barrels, boxes, jugs, canning jars, etc.)

3. Water heaters, toilet tanks, fish tanks, freezer ice, can all
   be used for sanitary or hygiene purposes, (Not for drinking)

4. Learn different types of treatment for water, i.e. boiling water,
   purification methods, filtration systems, etc.

5. Water for drinking purposes needs to be rotated every 6 -12
   months

6. Learn how to make a solar still

7. Set-up a safe and secure method of retrieving water

8. Identify resources of water in your surroundings, i.e. lakes,
   ponds, streams, rain barrels, etc.

9. Understand your surroundings and your climate whether it's
   Arizona (dry) or Alaska/Hawaii (wet)

10. Keep it simple, don't get overwhelmed and have FUN!

Water Storage Corner

Water: The Essential Nutrient

Water storage is probably the most important aspect of emergency preparedness. During any emergency, water is the first commodity found in short supply. A clean, reliable water source is vital, whether after an earthquake fire, and especially a flood; water will make or break a good emergency prepared plan.

Simply stated, one should provide a minimum of 2 quarts of clean drinking water/day for each adult, and lesser amounts for younger children and infants. For personal hygiene, 2 quarts of water, per person, per day is recommended. This need not necessarily be potable (drinkable), but free of pollutants and debris which could infect a cut or scratch or simply soil whatever is being washed or cleaned.

When one considers that a person normally uses in excess of 140 gallons of water/day for drinking, bathing, cooking etc., this really isn't that much water.

A 14 day supply of water, per person should be the first element of emergency storage. From a strictly survival point of view, water is the most important element for your body's survival and health. A person can lose all reserve carbohydrates and fat, and about half the body's protein without being in real danger. A loss of only 10-22% body weight as water is fatal.

The amount of water lost from the body through urination, water vapor from the lungs, sweating and through perspiration averages just about 2/3 gallon per day. Water loss must be made up by fluids consumed, and by the water produced in the body as a result of metabolic processes, and this doesn't mean soaking in a pool of water i.e., lake, bathtub etc.

Water: The Essential Nutrient

The effects of dehydration on the body are dramatic and life threatening. They range from thirst to stronger thirst, sleepiness, apathy, nausea, emotions instability, labored breathing and dizziness, to delirium and finally death.

Water Treatment

Caution:
Do not use water from toilet tanks containing colored disinfectant! Culinary (tap) water is what is normally stored for long term. If your containers are clean and opaque and are meant for water and the water is bacteria free, it can be stored for years and needn't be treated.

There is, however, no guarantee our culinary water is free of bacteria and should be tested to be sure before storing it for long periods. To be safe, the following
methods may be used to treat water for long term storage.

1) 2% Tincture of Iodine – Add 12 drops per gallon of water. Note: pregnant or nursing mothers or people with thyroid problems should not drink water with iodine

2) Chlorine Bleach – Household bleach can also be used. This should contain a 5.25% solution of sodium hypochlorite without soap additives, 5-8 drops per gallon.

Water Treatment

Long term use of iodine treated water can create health problems, so caution should be taken for use over long periods of time.

Another, more favorable type of water treatment /purification method and has other medicinal properties. It is stabilized oxygen called Ion that is very effective in killing bacteria without any harmful effects. In fact, it is very healthy.

For long term storage add 20 drops of Ion per gallon of water. One bottle will purify two 55 gallon drums of water. Bottles of Ion come in 2.33 oz bottles and is effective within about 2 ½ minutes. Ion can be obtained on the Internet at: waltonfeed.com then clicking on water storage supplies. Other web sources are available as well.

Do not use plastic bottles that have had milk or non-food products in them. Some plastics absorb the contents and will leach into water. Water should be stored in dark cool areas and/or in opaque containers. Inspect your water supply every few months.

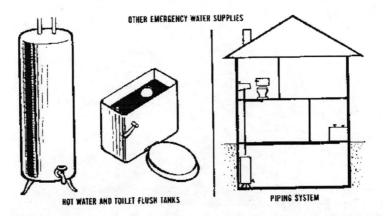

OTHER EMERGENCY WATER SUPPLIES

HOT WATER AND TOILET FLUSH TANKS   PIPING SYSTEM

Water Treatment

Water purification can be accomplished also by the following methods:

1) If water is cloudy, smelly, or other-wise polluted, strain it through a paper towel or several layers of clean cloth into a container in order to remove any sediment or flotsam.

2) Water that is boiled vigorously for five full minutes will usually be safe from harmful bacteria contamination.

3) If boiling is not possible, strain the water as indicated above and then add chlorine bleach or iodin as shown previously.

4) If bleach is a year old, the amount should be doubled. If 2 years or older, it shouldn't be used at all.

5) Other chemical treatments for water purification also included halzone tablets, iodine tablets or crystals. These tables can readily be found in drug and sporting goods stores.

6) If chlorine bleach is used, a sligh chlorine odor should be present.

Water Storage Corner

How to Store Water

The simplest way to store water is in 55 gallon, polyethylene (plastic) water drums. A simple and inexpensive hand pump that is inserted into the barrel will make it easy for water extraction. However, these barrels full of water are heavy and cannot be moved easily and unless the barrels are close to where the water will be used, it will require carrying amounts needed for cooking and hygiene. Therefore, the following are some additional suggestions for storing in smaller containers.

1) Two liter pop bottles, well cleaned
2) Sports, water drinking bottles
3) 5-15 gal. water containers; can be purchased in most stores
4) Canning jars filled and put thru a water-bath.

Remember also that you have other, in home, water containers where you may already have some water stored:

1) Water Heater
2) Toilet tanks
3) Water pipes and ice in the freezer

Portable Water Purification

A high quality filter system should possess the following characteristics:

1) Light-weight; have fewer parts (less to go wrong);

2) A fine pre-filter;

3) A replaceable or clearable filter;

4) Tight, well made pump;

5) high volume output;

6) Quick filtration;

7) Should screen out organisms over 0.5 microns (0.2 is best).

A system with all these features may not be inexpensive, however. A suggested source for water purification equipment is: www.travelerssupply.com or www.beprepared.com and their prices are quite reasonable.

Always use a filter properly. Use clearest water available (no water in a cow's hoof print), allowing suspended matter to settle out. Use a pre-filter if your system has one. Do not let outlet end of filter come in contact with contaminated Water. Be sure vessel you're pumping into is clean.

Emergency Water Procurement

In the event of natural or man-made disasters, wells, rivers, streams, lakes and public water sources are frequently poisoned or contaminated and are not reliable for obtaining water and should not be used until the water source can be tested for quality. Some different and maybe strange water sources are:

1) Roof water after a rain or snow
2) Canned food
3) Fish Tanks
4) Water beds
5) Solar panels and collectors
6) Ice cubes
7) Garden hoses
8) Swimming pools

Caution: Water from these sources should only be used for sanitary and hygiene purposes and highly filtered and treated if used for consumption.

After treating water by any method, it is best to let it stand for at least ½ hour and skimmed for any flotsam.

In winter, snow and ice from lakes or streams can be used, but should be boiled before human consumption. Never use swimming pool or water bed water for drinking or cooking as these have large amounts of chlorine in them.

Government agencies say it is safe to drink with 0.9 r. of radiation or less. This author does not recommend the consumption of any radioactive particles in con-tanimated water no matter what the level of radiation is.

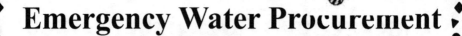

Emergency Water Procurement

You can survive several weeks without food. You can only survive a few days without water. The human body uses about ½ gallon per day under normal conditions, more in hot weather, but can survive on as little as 1 quart/day without total exhaustion and dehydration. In an emergency, never ration water, rather consume the required amount and then look for water tomorrow. Minimizing your activities and staying cool will conserve.

Salt intake should be minimized during hot weather to conserve body hydration.

Caution: Do not store water in empty bleach bottles. This increases the possibility of accidentally drinking full strength bleach. Also, after time the water stored becomes toxic.

Seal all water containers tight and store them in a cool, dark dry, well ventilated place. For water bed water storage, place two ounces of bleach per 100 gallons. Use water bed water for drinking water ONLY if other anti-bacterial chemicals or anti-mold/algae chemicals have NOT been added. Otherwise, use water bed water for hygiene purposes only.

Amount of bleach to use when purifying water

Amount of water	Clear Water	Cloudy Water
1 quart	2 drops	4 drops
1 gallon	8 drops	16 drops
5 gallons	½ teaspoon	1 teaspoon
55 gallons	5 ½ teaspoons	11 teaspoons

How To Make a Solar Still to Distill Water

Dig a hole about 18 inches deep and three feet wide square. Place a large #10 can in the bottom with a plastic tube or hose from the can out of the hole. Place vegetation in the bottom of the hole to induce moisture.

Cover the hole with clear plastic mounding dirt on the sides of the hole to hold the plastic in place. Place a small rock in the middle of the hole, over the can, on top of the plastic so that the condensation that will form in the hole on the underside of the plastic will run towards the middle an drip into the can. Check every several hours during the heat of the day for water in the can. Suck out the water with the hose.

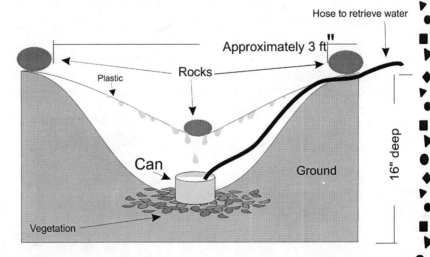

117

Water Storage Corner

Helpful Hints

Where as a quart of water per day, per person will sustain life, according to the Dept. of Defense and the Office of Civil Defense, it is recommended that a gallon of water per day per person be stored for food prep and drinking. A gallon provides added comfort and accommodates increased fluid needs at higher altitudes or warmer climates. An additional ½ to one gallon of water per day is recommended for bathing and hygiene, and to wash dishes.

Food-grade plastic containers are suitable for storing water. Stainless steel can be used to store water which has not been, or will not be treated with chlorine; chlorine is corrosive to most metals. Never use any metal containers that have had any type chemical stored in them. This goes for plastic containers as well.

Clearly label all water containers as water for drinking or hygiene; date them as well. Do not store water in direct sunlight.

Additionally, do not store water next to any gasoline, or other fuels or pesticides. Water stored properly has an indefinite shelf life; however, it is wise to replace water every 6-12 months.

If you have freezer space, storing some water in the freezer is a good idea. If you lose electrical power the ice will help in keeping food cold. Leave space in any container of water in the freezer as water expands when it freezes.

FAQ's - Emergency Water Supply

1. We live near a stream that runs year round. In the event of an emergency could we use water from the stream?

Answer: Under serious disaster conditions, no water can be presumed safe for consumption. Just because water is clear doesn't mean it is safe for drinking. Typhoid fever, dysentery, and infectious hepatitis are diseases associated with unsafe water. Water that has been exposed to animal feces may lead to cholera. The only way to guarantee a safe water supply is to store it away yourself, before a disaster.

2. How much water should I store?

Answer: This is a highly personal decision, but it is recommended that you store at least three days' worth of water for each member of each family--including pets. A minimum of one quart per day per person for survival. If you can, store more for a longer period of time.

FAQ's - Emergency Water Supply

3. How long can water be stored before it has to be rotated?

Answer: This is one of the most difficult questions to answer. The shelf life of this precious commodity depends on the original quality of the water, the temperature at which it is stored, how much light has it been exposed to, to just name a few. Many manufacturers of bottled water will include a shelf life on their product. It is suggested that it be rotated every 6-12 months.

4. Some of the water I have stored tastes flat, what should I do?

Answer: Stored water may eventually develop a disagreeable appearance, taste, or odor. Inspect your water supply at least every 6 months, sooner if possible just to be safe. Check for leaks and/or if any of the problems mentioned above have occurred, i.e. exposure to chemicals, light etc. Under emergency conditions, water that tastes flat can be aerated by pouring the water from one container to another and another three or four times. Water will lose its oxygen and this reintroduces the oxygen to the water.

Water Storage Corner

FAQ's - Emergency Water Supply

5. How can the shelf life of water be increased?

Answer: To increase the shelf life of water stored in opaque or translucent containers, group the containers together in dark plastic bags to keep out the light.

It isn't only sunlight that spoils water. Polyethylene plastics can be permeated by hydrocarbon vapors, so store your water supply away from any and all chemicals.

Short Term Water Storage

People who have electric pumps do draw water from their well have learned the lesson of filling up all available pots and pans when a thunderstorm is brewing. Unless, of course, as this author has, you have a generator hard wired to your home or a portable one that can readily be connected to the pump.

What would you do if you knew you would be losing electrical power in one hour?

Here are a couple options to filling pots and pans:

1. The simplest option is to put two or three heavy-duty plastic trash bags (avoid those with post-consumer recycled content) inside each other. Then fill the inner bag with water. You can use the trash can to give structure to the bag. (A great argument in keeping you trash containers clean!)

2. Fill your bath tubs with water. This is not for drinking, but for flushing toilets and washing. During winter months, fill your tubs with heaping mounds of snow. I say heaping, because snow, when melted will lose about 40% of its volume.

3. A home and all its plumbing, including the toilet, water heater and pipes, will store a significant amount of water. Be sure to close the valves to the outside as soon as possible to prevent the water from running back into the main line. It also prevents backwash of contaminated water into you're your house plumbing.

4. To access this water, first, open a faucet on the top floor. This will let air into the system so a vacuum doesn't hold the water in. Next, open a faucet in the basement. Gravity will take over and allow the water to drain out of your pipes into whatever container you have. You can repeat this procedure with both hot and cold water.

Water Storage Corner

Short Term Water Storage

and cold systems. Draining your hot water tank will work in the same manner by opening up its drain valve after opening a valve on the top floor of your house.

Most water heaters will have calc or other sediment in the bottom. This should not harm the water and can be cleaned by straining the water through a paper towel or other clean cloth.

Water Storage Corner

What to do if Caught with your Pants Down

There are certain climates and geographical locations where finding water will be quite easy (as in Alaska), or nearly impossible (Arizona desert). You'll have to take your location into account when you read the following:

Wherever you live, your best bet for finding water is to scout out suitable locations and stock up necessary equipment before an emergency strikes. When the time of need arrives, the time for preparation is long gone.

With proper preparedness, you should know not only the location of the nearest streams, springs or other water source but specific locations where it would be easy to fill a container and the safest run off from your roof or gutters.

Run off from roofs in desert locals shouldn't be relied upon. Getting the water safely back home should be examined. If there is a water shortage, other people will be looking for water too.

Scouting out good sources of water now, before an emergency, will bring you great comfort when/if an emergency hits you. "If ye are prepared, ye shall not fear."

Preparedness also means having at hand and easily installable system for collecting rain water and snow melt. This can range from large tarps or sheets of plastic to a system for collecting water run off from your roof or gutters. Always having a water barrel below your rain gutter down spout will assure a ready source of water in times of need without much effort.

What to do if Caught with your Pants Down

Those who live in desert areas won't have this luxury and will have to plan for other ways to find water. A hand pump well isn't a bad idea. This author has a hand pump well as well as an electric pump well system. This does NOT however, replace a water storage program for storing water. Once you have identified a source of water, you need to have containers ready. And, while you may think any water will do in a pinch, water that is not purified may make you sick, possibly even killing you. In a survival situation, with little or no medical attention available, you need to remain as healthy as possible and drinking bad water will not help and a bad case of the runs is very uncomfortable even in the best of times.

Boiling water is the best method of purifying water from natural water sources, i.e., streams, lakes etc. It doesn't require expensive equipment or chemicals, only a source of heat. Boiling water for at least 5-30 minutes will kill most common bacteria such as guardia & cryptosporidium. Boiling will not rid water of solid or foreign elements such as dirt, heavy metals or radiation.

Commercial filtering systems may also be obtained such as PUR or Katadyn are reasonably priced and easily obtainable. These filters range from small pump filters designed for backpackers and Texans who drink water from a cow's hoof print, to the larger sized filters designed for entire camps. For immediate survival needs, the model where you pour water into the top and allow it to slowly seep through the media into a cup in the bottom, is not too expensive and easily available for purchase.

On the down side, most such filtering devises for large amounts of water are a bit expensive and have a limited capacity. Filters are usually good from filtering 200 quarts to thousands of gallons, depending on the model and size of the filtering medium and mechanism. Some filters use fiberglass, activated charcoal,

What to do if Caught with your Pants Down

impregnated resin or ceramic elements. Read the label and choose the correct filter for your needs.

Chemicals (chlorine bleach, iodine etc.) are another choice but less suitable in some conditions and have limited shelf life.

Pour-through filtering systems can be made in an emergency. Here's an example of one that will remove many contaminants.

1. Take a 5 or 7 gallon pail (a 55 gallon barrel can be used for a large scale system) and drill or punch a series of small holes on the bottom.

2. Place several layers of cloth on the bottom of the pail, this can be anything from denim to an old table cloth; porous cloth.

3. Add a thick layer of sand (washed sand preferred) or loose pea gravel. This will be the main filtering element, so you should add at least half of the pail's depth.

4. Add another few layers of cloth, weighted down with some larger rocks.

5. This home made filter should now be several inches below the top rim of the pail you are using.

6. Place another pail or collection device under the holes in the bottom of your filtering pail.

7. Pour the water you have collected into the top of your filtering pail. As gravity works its magic, the water will filter down through the sand/gravel and layers of cloth and drip out the bottom, into your collecting container. If the water is cloudy you can simply

What to do if Caught with your Pants Down

filter it again, or let it stand for 30 or so minutes and collect the water that is on the top through a straw or hose.

Helpful Hint

You can obtain some activated charcoal from your local aquarium supplies store and add a layer of the charcoal inside the filter you have made. Place a layer of cloth above and especially below the charcoal. This will remove other contaminants and improve taste as well. This filtering system works well with relatively clean water. Once the system has been used, change the sand/gravel regularly.

Water Storage Corner

American Red Cross Information

The American Red Cross suggests that all Americans everywhere should store water, even if you live in areas where a disaster is less likely to strike, ie., floods, earthquakes, tornados, wildfires, hurricanes and war. We never know when a natural or man-made disaster will strike, so store water even if you think you don't need to.

The American Red Cross recommends the use of directions provided by your local or state public health agency. In the case where state or local health agency does not provide public information, follow these few simple steps provided in this book. Much other information is available on the internet. Water storage for emergency purposes isn't rocket science.

If your local water is not treated commercially by a water treatment facility, that is, if your water comes from a public well or other public, not-treated system, follow instructions about water storage found in this book.

Treating commercially-treated water with bleach or some other chemical is super-fluous and not necessary. Doing so does not increase storage life. It is important to change and replace stored water every 6-12 months or more frequently.

For more information, contact your local American Red Cross chapter and ask for the brochure titled: "Food and Water in an Emergency" (A5055)

www.redcross.org/services/disaster

Water Storage Summary

Let's summarize what we've talked about

1. One gallon of water per person per day
2. Children, nursing mothers, and sick people may need more water
3. In hot climates, more water is needed
4. Store water tightly and in clean plastic containers, out of the light and keep cool and store away from chemicals
5. Keep at least a three day supply of water per person
6. Long term storage can be kept in 55 gallon plastic drums; rotate 6-12 mos
7. Short term storage can be kept in 2 liter pop bottles and other such bottles
8. Treat water with iodine, chlorine bleach and water tablets. Long term storage with chemicals can create health problems, so chemically treated water should be rotated often.
9. Locate and acquire water filtering devices.
10. Scout out natural water sources in case of emergency.
11. Locate water sources stored in home plumbing etc.
12. Learn to make a water solar still
13. Learn where and how to contact your local and state emergency agencies

Additional web-sites for more water storage containers, filters and water treatment chemicals are shown below.

www.beprepared.com
www.disasternecesities.com
www.gemplers.com

First Aid Corner

"Can you save a life"?

First Aid Corner

Simple steps to help you in this corner:

1. Learn CPR - Save a Life

2. Learn how to treat burns

3. Learn how to treat wounds

4. Learn how to create a tourniquet and when to use it

5. Learn how to control bleeding

6. Learn how to control a nose bleed

7. Learn how to treat shock

8. Learn how to treat fractures, sprains and strains

9. Learn how to use and what types of splints

10. Find out how to get involved in your community

First Aid Corner

Rescue Breathing & CPR

Can You Save A Life?

Not many of us will ever be presented with a life threatening situation where we have to administer First-Aid, however, there may be times when we will be happy we know some First-Aid. The aid we give will be first. Helping another human being when they are injured or in peril of losing their life is disconcerting to anyone who is not a medically trained professional; even physicians and EMT's (Emergency Medical Technicians) say they are disturbed by emergency medical issues.

This **Corner** is not all inclusive or comprehensive in First-Aid. However, we are going to provide some basic information for anyone to follow to render that all needed aid … first. You can help someone in an emergency if you know what to do.

RESCUE BREATHING & CPR

(Cardio Pulmonary Resuscitation)

This section is to give guidance for assisting a person who is unconscious and not breathing. If you are the one administering rescue breathing or CPR and another person is available, have them call 9-1-1 while you are administering to the victim. If you are alone, before doing anything, call 9-1-1. The sooner you call, the sooner help arrives. Besides, you might forget how to administer rescue breathing and/or CPR and operators can assist you through the procedures until help arrives. Begin rescue breathing or CPR immediately. The following are some guidelines to assist in administering rescue breathing & CPR.

First Aid Corner

Rescue Breathing & CPR

Rescue Breathing For Those Age 1 Year Through Adult

· First, try to rouse the person. Say, "Open your eyes!" or "Talk to me!" while gently shaking the person's shoulders.

· If there is no response, remember your ABC's – A for airway, B for breathing, C for circulation. First, open the airway. Second, provide rescue breathing. Third, if you don't see signs of movement – use CPR to support circulation and keep life-sustaining blood and oxygen moving around the person's body. (CPR discussion is next section)

· Roll the person into a face-up position. With one of your hands on the person's forehead and the fingers of the other under the chin, lift up, and gently lean the person's head back so the chin points up.

· If the person's head is at an odd angle, suspect a neck (spinal) injury. Open the airway by gently lifting the person's jaw, but don't tilt the head back. That might aggravate any spinal or neck injury.· .

· Look, listen for signs of breathing; chest rising and falling or breath sounds.

· To give rescue breathing, keep person's head tilted back and the airway open. Pinch the person's nostrils tightly shut to keep air from escaping.

· Take a deep breath. Position your mouth around the person's open mouth, creating a tight seal. When possible, use a barrier device available at medical supply stores. This protects you and the patient as well.

· Blow into person's mouth for about two seconds, until you

First Aid Corner

Rescue Breathing & CPR

- the chest rise.

- If you don't see the chest rise, try repositioning the person's head – lift the chin, tilt the head back. If rescue breathing still doesn't raise the chest, assume there's an airway obstruction. With the person lying face-up, you can't perform the Heimlich maneuver. But, you can do something similar that has the same effect: Kneel, straddling the person's hips. Place one hand on top of the other below the rib cage, and give abdominal thrusts to dislodge any object blocking the airway. When obstructing material pops free, remove it, then look and listen. If you detect no signs of breathing, begin rescue breathing again.

- After blowing into the person's mouth, remove yours. Keep the person's nose pinched, mouth open and chin up. Allow the chest to fall – this takes about 2 seconds.

- Repeat mouth-to-mouth breathing every five seconds with the person's chest visibly rising, then falling.

- Check for normal breathing or other signs of independent breathing – chest rising and falling, coughing, movement.

- If breathing returns, place the person in the recovery position (see illustration below). Kneel beside the person. Grasp the arm nearest you. Extend it and bend it at the elbow into a right angle. Grasp the other arm. Pull it toward you, positioning the back of the hand against the cheek nearest you. Extend the person's leg nearest you. Bend the other leg at the knee. Holding the raised knee and the hand by the cheek, roll the person toward you, into a side-lying position. Tilt the person's head slightly back to keep the airway open. The recovery position allows liquids to drain from the person's mouth, and helps prevent inhalation of anything that comes up from the stomach. It's

First Aid Corner

Rescue Breathing & CPR

- stable enough to allow you to leave the person unattended for awhile to get help.

- After a minute or two of rescue breathing, if you see no signs of circulation – breathing , coughing, movement – begin CPR.

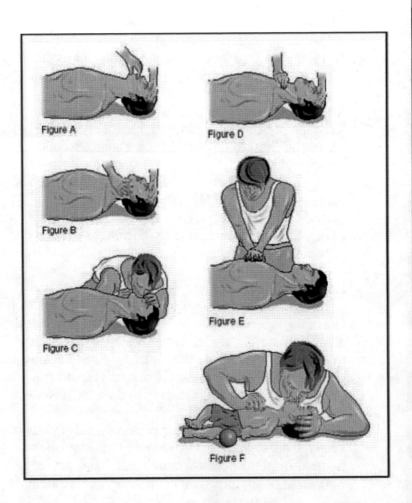

First Aid Corner

Rescue Breathing & CPR

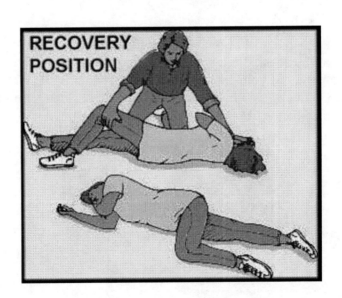

First Aid Corner

Rescue Breathing & CPR

For Infants Under Age 1

Rescue breathing is the same as for adults except:

- Never shake an infant. Instead, try to rouse the baby by tapping or tickling the sole of a foot

- With a baby, don't pinch the nostrils. Place your mouth over the baby's mouth and nose; blow gently

- The infant rescue position involves placing baby on a table or cradling the baby in your arms with the head tilted somewhat downward to reduce the risk of choking

CPR For Adults

For those age 9 through adult: Position the person face-up, as you would for rescue breathing. Kneel to one side of the person's chest.

- Place the heel of one hand on top of the other in the center of the chest, directly between the nipples. Interlock the fingers of your first hand into the second. Pull you fingers up and press with the heel of your hand. This minimizes the chance of breaking ribs. See illustration below.

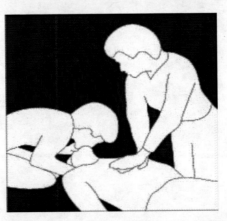

First Aid Corner

Rescue Breathing & CPR

- With your arms straight, lean over person and press straight down firmly on the breastbone so it goes down 1 ½ to 2 inches. After each compression, allow the chest to rise completely before repeating.
- Perform 15 chest compressions at the rate of 100 per minute.
- Then tilt head, lift chin; give two mouth-to-mouth rescue breaths.
- Repeat the cycle of 15 chest compressions and 2 rescue breaths until emergency medical help arrives, or until you're too exhausted to continue.

For children age 1 through 8

- Perform CPR as you would for an adult, but use only the heel of one hand for chest compressions.
- Press down firmly on the chest so that it falls 1 to 1 ½ inches.
- Perform 5 chest compressions, about 2 per second.
- Then give 1 rescue breath.
- Repeat the cycle of 5 chest compressions and 1 rescue breath until emergency medical help takes over, or the child takes a breach or starts to move, or until you're too exhausted to continue, or your safety is at risk and there will be two people to rescue.

For infants under 1

- Instead of using the heel of your hand, use the tips of your index and middle fingers. Place them on the breastbone between the baby's nipples.

First Aid Corner

Rescue Breathing & CPR

- Press down firmly on the chest so that it falls ½ to ¾ inch.
- Perform 5 chest compressions, about 2 per second
- Then give 1 rescue breath, covering the baby's nose and mouth with your mouth
- Repeat the cycle of 5 chest compressions and 1 rescue breath until emergency medical help takes over, or the infant takes a breath or starts to move.

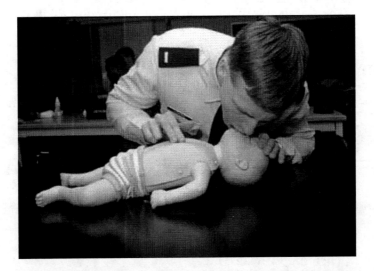

The best way to learn lifesaving first-aid is to take a class. The American Red Cross offers comprehensive first-aid training. Find a local CERT (Citizens Emergency Response Team) chapter and take their training class. In some communities, police and fire departments offer CPR and first-aid training.

First Aid Corner

Treating Burns

The object of treating burns is to stop the burning and cover to reduce pain and infection. Burns may be caused by heat, chemicals, electrical current, and radiation. The severity of a burn depends on many factors – the temperature of the burning agent, the period of time that the victim was exposed, the area of the body that is burned, how much area is affected, the age of the victim, and the burn depth.

Burn Classifications

The skin contains three layers;

- Epidermis. The outer layer of the skin. This layer contains nerves and hair.
- Dermis. The middle layer of skin. This layer contains blood vessels, oil glands, hair follicles, and sweat glands.
- Subcutaneous. The innermost layer of skin. This layer contains blood vessels and overlies the muscle and skin cells.

Depending on the severity, burns may affect all three layers of skin. The critical areas of the body for burns are the:

- Face
- Hands
- Feet
- Genitalia

First Aid Corner

Burn Classifications

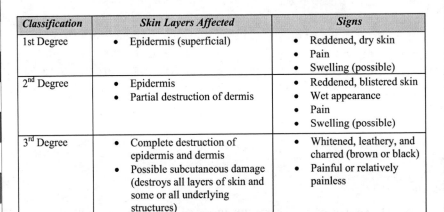

Classification	Skin Layers Affected	Signs
1st Degree	• Epidermis (superficial)	• Reddened, dry skin • Pain • Swelling (possible)
2nd Degree	• Epidermis • Partial destruction of dermis	• Reddened, blistered skin • Wet appearance • Pain • Swelling (possible)
3rd Degree	• Complete destruction of epidermis and dermis • Possible subcutaneous damage (destroys all layers of skin and some or all underlying structures)	• Whitened, leathery, and charred (brown or black) • Painful or relatively painless

Burn Treatment

First-aid treatment for burn victims involves removing the source of the burn, cooling the burn, and covering it. Some guidelines for treating burns include:

- Remove the victim from the burn source. Put out any flames and remove smoldering clothing.
- If skin or clothing is still hot, cool them by immersing in cool water for not longer than 1 minute or covering with clean compresses that have been wrung out in cool water. Possible cooling sources include water from the bathroom or kitchen; garden hose; and soaked towels, sheets, or other cloths. Use only clean water. For 3rd degree burns, do not apply water except to put out flames. Treat all 3rd degree victims for shock. (See **Treatment For Shock** at the end of this section.)
- Cover loosely with dry, sterile dressings to keep air out,
- reduce pain, and prevent infection.
- Elevate burned extremities higher than the heart.

Burn Treatment

When Treating Burns:

- **<u>Do not</u>** use ice, which can cause hypothermia. If you burn your finger on a hot stove and the burn is very minor, placing an ice cube on the burn for a few minutes will reduce pain significantly and is O.K.
- **<u>Do not</u>** apply antiseptics, ointments, or other remedies such as butter or lard.
- **<u>Do not</u>** remove shreds of tissue, break blisters, or remove adhered particles of clothing. (Cut burned-in clothing around the burn.)

With younger people, older people and people with sever burns, use caution when applying cool dressings. These people are more susceptible to hypothermia. After a sever burn, chills may set it so they may need to be covered with a blanket. A rule of thumb is do not cool more than fifteen percent of body surface area (the size of one arm) at once, to prevent hypothermia.

First Aid Corner

Treating Wounds

The objectives of first-aid treatment for wounds is to control bleeding and prevent secondary infection. Cleaning and bandaging help to prevent infection. First, clean the wound by irrigating with clean water, then flushing with a mild concentration of soap & tepid water, then irrigating with clean water again. ***Do Not Scrub!*** A bulb syringe or hypodermic syringe is useful for irrigating wounds. After thoroughly cleaning the wound, you will need to apply a dressing * and bandage* to help keep the wound dry and clean.

* Note: A *dressing* is applied directly to the wound. A *bandage* is used to hold the dressing in place.

To dress and bandage, clean the wound area as described above, place a sterile dressing directly to the wound, and apply a bandage to hold it in place. If the wound is still bleeding, the bandage should place enough pressure on the wound to help control bleeding without interfering with circulation. **Check** for color, warmth, and sensation to determine if the bandage is too tight. If the skin is white, this means the capillaries (tiny blood vessels) are not refilling with blood; you will need to loosen the bandage

Use the following rules for dressings and bandages:

- In the absence of active bleeding, dressings must be removed and the wound flushed and checked for signs of infection at least every 4 to 6 hours. Signs of possible infection include:
    1. Swelling around the wound site
    2. Discoloration
    3. Discharge (puss) from the wound
    4. Red striations from the wound site

Treating Wounds
& Amputations

- If there is active bleeding (the dressing and bandage soaked in blood), redress <u>over</u> the existing dressing and maintain pressure and elevation.

AMPUTATIONS

Amputations are wounds of a very severe nature. They are defined as a severing of a limb or other body part. I am only going to cover this subject briefly as these type of wounds need very expert treatment, but if you are faced with an amputation wound, this information will give you some knowledge of what aid to give first until trained medical help is available or you get the victim to the hospital.

To treat the victim, control bleeding, watch for signs of shock, and treat for shock as necessary (See **Treatment For Shock** at the end of this section). If a part of the body is severed and can be found, save tissue parts, wrapped in clean material, in a plastic bag if available, and keep the tissue parts cool. Keep the severed part with the victim.

Obviously, a severed body part will bleed profusely. Therefore, controlling the bleeding is paramount in any amputation, if not, the victim will surely die. If bleeding cannot be controlled by pressure bandaging, a tourniquet may be necessary. A tourniquet is *rarely* required and should be used only as a *last resort* – a "life or limb" situation. Tourniquets are considered appropriate treatment for crushing type injuries and for partial amputations. Using a tourniquet can pose serious risks to the affected limb, so it should not be used unless *not* using it will endanger the person's life from excessive blood loss. The most serious dangers in tourniquet use stem from :

Amputations

- *Incorrect materials or application,* which increases the damage and bleeding. If narrow materials (such as wire or twine) are used or the tourniquet is too tight, nerves, blood vessels and muscles may be damaged.
- *Damage to the limb from a tourniquet.* Survival of a limb is almost never possible after a correctly applied tourniquet is left on too long. Only a physician should remove a tourniquet. If you apply a tourniquet, leave it in plain sight, do not cover it with a bandage. Attach an adhesive label to the victim's forehead stating the time the tourniquet was applied.

TOURNIQUET

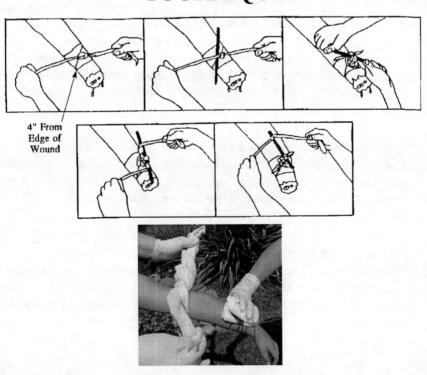

4" From Edge of Wound

First Aid Corner

Controlling Bleeding

Uncontrolled bleeding initially causes weakness. If bleeding is not controlled within a short period, the victim will go into shock (described at the end of this section), and finally die. The average adult holds about 5 liters of blood. Because the loss of just 1 liter poses a risk of death, it is critical that excessive bleeding be controlled in the shortest amount of time possible.

There are three main types of bleeding. The type can usually be identified by how fast the blood flows.

- *Arterial Bleeding* — Arteries transport blood under high pressure. Therefore, bleeding from an artery is *spurting bleeding* and the most serious.
- *Venous Bleeding* — Veins transport blood under low pressure. Bleeding from a vein is *flowing bleeding.*
- *Capillary Bleeding* — Capillaries also carry blood under low pressure. Bleeding from capillaries is *oozing bleeding.*

Use the table below for one or a combination of methods for controlling bleeding.

Method	Procedures
Direct Local Pressure	• Place direct pressure over the wound by putting a clean pad over the wound and pressing firmly. • Maintain compression by wrapping the wound firmly with a pressure bandage.
Elevation	• Elevate the wound above the level of the heart.
Pressure Points	• Put pressure on the nearest pressure point to slow the flow of blood to the wound. A pressure point is a pulse point for a major artery. Use the: ■ Brachial point for bleeding in the arm ■ Femoral point for bleeding in the leg * Note: See pressure points in illustration below

First Aid Corner

Controlling Bleeding

Ninety-five percent of bleeding can be controlled by direct pressure combined with elevating the wound above the heart.

Know the pressure points shown in the illustration below. These points are chosen because there is a bone or hard tissue over which he artery passes. When you press your hand against the bone or harder tissue, you flatten out the artery, much like pinching a hose or rubber tube to stop the flow of water. Don't press too hard. If the bleeding does not stop, you may be pressing on the wrong pressure point or pressing in the wrong direction. Most of our first-aid experiences will be dealing with minor injuries and cuts – cut fingers, scraped knees that happen frequently. However, even they need attention.

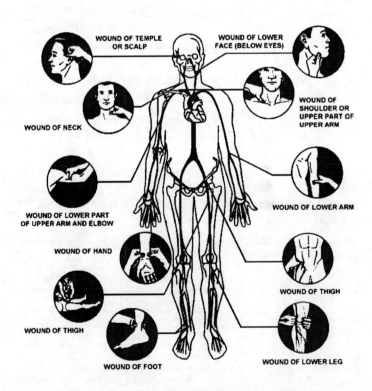

WOUND OF TEMPLE OR SCALP

WOUND OF LOWER FACE (BELOW EYES)

WOUND OF NECK

WOUND OF SHOULDER OR UPPER PART OF UPPER ARM

WOUND OF LOWER PART OF UPPER ARM AND ELBOW

WOUND OF LOWER ARM

WOUND OF HAND

WOUND OF THIGH

WOUND OF THIGH

WOUND OF FOOT

WOUND OF LOWER LEG

First Aid Corner

Treating Nose Bleeds

Every parent has had a child come running in with a nose bleed. Nose bleeds can be caused by a punch in the nose by the neighborhood bully or some other blow to the nose. A skull fracture may cause the nose to bleed. Sometimes, even non-trauma-related conditions such as sinus infection, high blood pressure and dry climates or bleeding disorders will cause nose bleeds. Sometimes they are difficult to get stopped.

Don't underestimate nose bleeds' seriousness. They can lead to shock if not controlled. The actual blood loss may not be readily evident because much blood can go down the throat and be swallowed. A victim who has swallowed a lot of blood may become nauseated and vomit. Vomitus (what comes up from the stomach), if aspirated (breathed or sucked into the lungs) will result in serious complications

To control nosebleeds caused by injuries to the nose:

- · Control bleeding by:
    - Pinching the nostrils together
    - Putting pressure on the upper lip just under the nose (e.g., place rolled gauze between the upper lip and gum and press against it with the fingers)

- · Have the victim sit with the head slightly forward so that blood trickling down the throat will not be breathed into the lungs. Do *not* put the head back.

- · Be sure the victim's airway remains open.

- · Keep the victim quiet. Anxiety will increase the blood flow by raising blood pressure.

First Aid Corner

Treatment For Shock

Shock is a serious medical condition caused by the body not getting enough blood flow, which means vital organs are not receiving enough oxygen and nutrients to function properly so they shut down.

Treatment for shock in first-aid conditions are managed by an acronym "WARTS" W=Warmth; **A**=ABC's(Airway, Breathing, Circulation or CPR); R=Rest and reassurance; T=Treatment (treat the cause of shock); S=Semi-prone position, which is the same thing as recovery position). The following guidelines will assist you in treating shock:

- Immediately provide a comfortable position for the victim if they are conscious
- If you are alone, call for help. If not, send someone to call 9-1-1 and have someone stay with the victim
- Ensure airway is clear and that the victim is breathing. If possible, place victim in recovery position
- Apply direct pressure to a bleeding wound
- Cover victim with a blanket or jacket, but not too thick to cause over heating
- Do not give victim a drink, but do moisten the lips if requested
- If legs are uninjured, elevate them 12 – 15 inches
- Reassure the victim as they will be anxious, frightened and possibly nauseated
- Prepare for CPR if conditions might require it be administered
- If the victim is conscious and lucid, ask them questions like: "Do you have a medical condition? What happened? Do you take medications, if so what? Do you have any allergies to medication?" Record this information and give to the ambulance or medical personnel if the victim becomes unconscious.

First Aid Corner

Treatment For Shock

The management of shock requires immediate intervention, even before a diagnosis is made. Re-establishing blood flow to the organs is the primary goal through restoring and maintaining blood circulation volume.

- Place the victim in shock position
- Keep the person warm and comfortable
- Turn the victim's head to one side if neck injury is not suspected

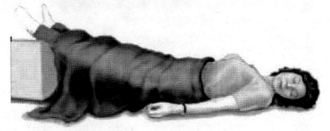

Recognizing Shock In Someone

As stated, shock is a disorder resulting from a severe injury (less sever injuries may also result in shock) caused by ineffective circulation of blood. Remaining in shock will lead to the death of cells, tissues, and entire organs. Immediate treatment is necessary.

Initially, the body will compensate for blood loss, so signs of shock may not appear immediately. It is important, therefore, to continually evaluate and monitor a victim's condition. Observable symptoms of shock to look for are:

- Rapid, shallow breathing (rate greater than 30/minute)
- Cold, pale skin (capillary refill greater than 2 seconds) *
- Failure to respond to simple commands, such as "Squeeze my hand."

* Note: Capillary refill can be tested by pressing a finger on the inside of the arm and releasing quickly to see how fast color returns to the skin.

First Aid Corner

Treating Fractures, Sprains And Strains

The objective when treating a suspected fracture, sprain or strain is to immobilize the injury and the joints immediately above and immediately below the injury site. Because there are several different types of injuries and your actions depend in part on the type of injury encountered, this section will describe the different types of injuries possible.

FRACTURES

A fracture is a complete break, chip or crack in a bone. Fractures are classified as:

- **Closed**   A broken bone with no associated wound. First-Aid may only require splinting.

- **Open**   A broken bone with some kind of wound that allows contaminants to enter into or around the fracture site. Open fractures are more dangerous because of the risk of severe bleeding and infection. They are, therefore, a higher priority injury and should be checked more frequently. When treating an open fracture:

    - Do *not* draw the exposed bone ends back into the tissue.

    - Cover the wound with a sterile dressing. Do not irrigate the wound

    - Cover the exposed bone with a moist 4 X 4 bandage to keep it from drying out.

    - Splint the fracture without disturbing the wound.

First Aid Corner

Treating Fractures, Sprains And Strains

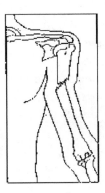   

Displaced Fracture   **Nondisplaced Fracture**   **Closed Fracture**   **Open Fracture**

Closed fractures may be described by the degree of displacement of the bone fragments. If the limb is angled, then there is a *displaced fracture.* A displaced fracture may be detected by seeing and feeling the deformity. A *non-displaced fracture* is difficult to identify without X-rays. The main indicators are usually pain and swelling, which could also indicate a strain or sprain. Therefore, treat areas where there is pain and swelling as a suspected fracture until a professional medical diagnosis and care can be obtained.

Another condition closely related to a sprain or strain, and sometimes confused as a fracture, is the dislocation. A dislocation is an injury to the ligaments around a joint that is so severe that it results in separation of the bone from its normal position at a joint. Once dislocated, the bones lock in their new position. The joints most commonly dislocated are fingers, shoulders, elbows, hips and ankles. The signs of dislocation are similar to those of a fracture, so treat a suspected dislocation like a fracture -- immobilize.

As with a broken bone, if you suspect a dislocation, do *not* attempt to relocate the joint. Immobilize the joint until it can be treated by a trained medical person.

First Aid Corner

Sprains And Strains

A sprain is the stretching or tearing of ligaments at a joint and is usually caused by stretching or extending the joint beyond its normal range of motion. A sprain is considered a partial dislocation, although (unlike a full dislocation) the bone is able to fall back into place after the injury. The joints most easily sprained are the ankle, knee, wrist and fingers. Common symptoms of sprains include:

· Tenderness at the site of the injury
· Swelling and/or bruising
· Restricted use, or loss of use of the joint and range of motion

Because the signs of a sprain are similar to those of a non-displaced fracture, do *not* attempt to treat the injury beyond immobilization and elevation.

A strain is the stretching and tearing of muscles or tendons, rather than ligaments. Strains most often involve the muscles in the neck, back, thigh or calf. In some cases, a strain is indistinguishable from a sprain or fracture without X-rays or other, more sophisticated diagnostic methods. In these cases, treat the injury as a fracture. When treating fractures, sprains or strains (and dislocations, possibly) remove shoes, tight clothing and jewelry such as rings, watches etc., from the injured area to prevent these items from acting as a tourniquet if swelling occurs. Ever tried to get a ring off a swollen finger?

154

First Aid Corner

Splinting

I determined that it doesn't do any good to talk about fractures, sprains and strains if we don't also discuss different methods of splinting/immobilizing an injured body part. Splinting is the most common method for immobilization in emergency conditions. A variety of materials may be used for first-aid splinting. Typically, cardboard is used until professional care can be obtained. However, other materials that may be available can also be used, such as:

- *Soft Materials*   A towel can be rolled into a thick tube shape, placed around the injury and secured in several places with bandaging materials or even duct tape.

- *Rigid Materials*   A board or stick, metal strip, folded magazine or newspaper or other rigid item may be used to support the injured part and secure with bandaging materials or strong twine.

- *Anatomical Splint*   A fractured bone can be secured to an adjacent, unfractured bone by binding the two together in several places (for example, two fingers or two legs).

Some helpful guidelines for placing and checking splints include:

- Support the injured area above and below the injury, including the joints
- If possible, splint the injury in the position you find it
- Don't try to realign bones or joints, leave this to professional medical personnel
- After splinting, check for proper circulation (warmth, feeling, color)

First Aid Corner

Splinting

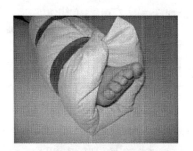 

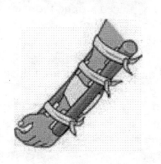 

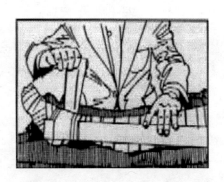 

First Aid Corner

Conclusion

In other **Corners** of this book you will find more information relating to emergency preparedness that will be helpful in First-Aid situations. I would like to strongly suggest that you not only read and study the information in this book, but also seek out some First-Aid training through your neighborhood or community CERT or Red Cross agencies. If, in your community, there is no CERT or Red Cross organization which trains people in First-Aid and other emergency preparedness, perhaps you could contact them to start your own chapter in your community. Knowledge is always a good thing and can be very useful, especially if there are others around you who are trained and willing to help during an emergency.

The need for disaster medical/First-Aid operations is based on two assumptions:

- The number of victims will exceed the local capacity for treatment.
- Survivors will assist others. They will do whatever they know how to do. They need to know lifesaving or post-disaster survival techniques.

This being said, any and all who have some training in emergency and First-Aid training will be worth their weight in gold. So, get some training. Join CERT or begin a chapter in your area. You can go online to: www.citizencorps.gov/cert and learn how to get involved in and receive training.

Much of this **Corner** was taken directly out of and quoted from the CERT Participant Handbook. So, to end this **Corner,** let's get 'er done!

Communication & Family Location Corner

Communication & Family Location Corner

Simple steps to help you with this corner

1. During a disaster, communication is vital; keep lines of communication with emergency services and family
2. Purchase/acquire means of communication i.e., battery or crank operated radio with frequencies for emergency channels; acquire Walkie Talkies or other radios such as CB or Ham radio; acquire skills to use them
3. Learn radio requirements for Ham radio license; learn other communication methods i.e., Morse Code, semaphore and flashlight
4. Prepare a family location plan; be sure to provide all family members with contact numbers and central gathering place for all; plan for backup location
5. When verbal or other communication is not available, learn some basic search and rescue skills; join CERT; join Red Cross or other organizations to assist you and your community
6. Keep emergency pack with radios or Walkie Talkies handy in case of quick evacuation is needed; post emergency numbers by telephones for all to see
7. Learn CPR and first aid skills; receive or attend training updates
8. Become familiar with and teach family members to always carry communication aids while in the wild; learn to communicate with air search personnel in airplanes
9. Learn basic tracking and ground signals for aircraft searchers; understand aircraft signals; learn to read a compass and/or (use a pin or needle to make your own compass) map and find directions by stars and your watch
10. Keep it simple, don't get overwhelmed and have FUN!

Communication

After certification with CERT (Citizens Emergency Response Team) it was all too well obvious that one of the most serious problems in dealing with an emergency or disaster, is communication. Communication break downs, not only among citizens/families, but between emergency support systems, ie., fire department, police, search and rescue, volunteer teams such as CERT. Not necessarily between the emergency support teams, but between citizens/families and the emergency support teams.

Communication between those needing emergency assistance/rescue and those agencies in charge of fighting natural or man-mad disasters is, of course, vital and essential, but the focus of this **CORNER** is the all too important communication between family members and being able to establish and keep communication lines open during emergency situations.

Disasters come without warning……..usually. I say usually, because there may be times when floods can be predicted or wildfires and even war. However, most of the time, disasters come without warning. We have to remember that we, as a modern society, have become accustomed to just picking up a cell phone

Communication & Family Location Corner

Communication

and calling, not thinking or realizing that cell phones require transmission (cell) towers to send the signal to the person being called. During disasters, natural and man-made, those "cell" towers can become damaged or destroyed, making cell phone inoperative. Even land-line phones have to have a communication link by wire, above and below ground. So, land-line phones are even subject to being inoperative.

A typical, or even not so typical, family will have children in school during the winter months. Mom may or may not be employed outside the home and dad will be away from the home at work during the day. So, our homes could be occupied by mom and younger children who are not in school, or even empty; every- one away at school, work or all together on a trip when disaster occurs. Typically, families are not all together in the home except during evening and sleeping hours. However, when some or all of the family members are away from the home, there needs to be a plan in place, familiar to all members of the family, to be able to communicate with one another in the event of a disaster. This plan should include a meeting place away from home if the home is destroyed or you can't get home.

Communication

Let's say dad and children are away at work and school, and mom is home alone. An earthquake strikes, destroying telephone lines and cell phone towers. The streets are all broken up, travel, even by four-wheel drive vehicles is difficult. Dad can't call home, his cell and office phones are inoperable, the school phones and the house phones are also out. Mom is frantic, wondering what has happened to dad and the children. Electricity is out, so television is not available. (With this scenario in mind, this is the time to consider having a battery powered AM/FM radio available. Be sure to have extra batteries available. A hand crank radio removes the need for batteries) Even if dad's place of business has a plan to evacuate their place of business, mom has no clue whether dad is ok, if he needs help, or if he can make it home.

Communication & Family Location Corner

Communication

Schools generally have evacuation plans in an emergency and have drills to practice, so unless the school is totally destroyed, the school administrators will keep the children at the school until parents can be located. Some schools even have radios for emergency use. Schools will try to unite children and parents.

But, what if you have teenagers who are away from home, not necessarily at school? What if some of your family lives far distances from you and are affected by the same disaster, ie. grand earthquake or war? Not knowing is frightening to anyone, especially parents and children.

Communication & Family Location Corner

Communication

During the Alaska Earthquake (registered at 9.2 on the Richter Scale) in 1964, this writer was a Junior in High School. And, as luck (or fate) would have it, was away from home as well. I hung onto a tree to keep from falling down. Buildings collapsed around me, streets opened up, buildings fell into deep chasms and all this lasted over five minutes, not for just a few seconds as most quakes. Needless to say, all telephone communication was out of order, and all other utilities were out as well. Being away from home was very disconcerting, but not being able to communicate with family was quite terrifying as it was not known if the family home was destroyed, or other siblings injured … or whether or not I could even get back home with so much damage. Because of all the confusion and vehicles not being able to drive on many roads, it took me several hours to find my way home.

Communication & Family Location Corner

Communication Devices

Thankfully our home was intact, only a large crack in the foundation, but there were no utilities whatsoever. Fortunately, my father was a fanatic for home/emergency preparedness and we were able to survive quite comfortably for the next two weeks until power and other utilities were restored to our area of Anchorage. We even had enough to help our neighbors who weren't prepared. The point of all this, is that I was away from home and my younger brother was out delivering newspapers. He continued delivering papers and it took me several hours to walk home. My mother was very worried because, even though we were prepared for survival, we did not have a communication plan.

In 1964 there were no cell phones. It isn't even certain that the cell phone towers would have withstood the quaking anyway. We did not, as a family, have any plan for communicating or a plan to meet at a certain location in the even of a disaster. In 1964, they did have large hand-held radios, but who wants to carry around a big heavy radio everywhere they go? I don't, and you probably don't either.

Today, cell phones are a convenient and easy method of staying in touch … so long as they are still working. When cell towers go down, you're out of luck. Nowadays, technology is such, that small, convenient and reasonably priced radios can be carried in an emergency pack that we all should have in our cars. Some small, Walkie Talkie type radios called FRS (Family Radio Services) can be operated without a license because their range is short, usually around 1-3 miles. They are relatively inexpensive and are sold in sporting goods stores, hardware stores and many other stores. These type radios are typically used by hunters, hikers and skiers or others who want to remain in contact with one another when in places such as carnivals, expos, fairs, rodeos and other places where one might become separated from family or friends. They are user friendly and inexpensive to operate, using regular batteries

Communication Devices

or rechargeable batteries.

Hand held radios that have significant range require a license and range in price from just a couple hundred dollars on up. When communication is desired between family members when separated by long distances, it might also be advisable to have what is called a home based transceiver to be able to communicate with whomever is left at home.

Ham radios come in different classes of use, from the very amateur, to the advanced Ham radio operator. Ham radios can reach all the way around the world. Remember, once you advance beyond Walkie Talkie type radios, you need a license. CB (Citizen Band) radios are the exception. In some locations, CB radios can reach quite a long distance. CB radios once used to be very popular to have in one's automobile, but now, it is mostly the ware of the trucking industry. If you live in a small community with few obstructions, a home based CB and a CB in all automobiles used by family members would be an inexpensive way to stay in touch in case of a disaster ... unless of course, the disaster destroyed the automobile or the home. It is virtually impossible to prepare for all eventualities. Prepare for the worst and hope for the best. The following page will show a list of the National 10-codes used by the trucking industry.

Communication & Family Location Corner

Communication Devices

10-1	Receiving poorly	10-33	Emergency Traffic
10-2	Receiving well	10-34	Trouble at this station
10-3	Stop transmitting	10-35	Confidential information
10-4	OK, message received	10-36	Correct time is ....
10-5	Relay message	10-37	Wrecker needed at ....
10-6	Busy, stand by	10-38	Ambulance needed at ..
10-7	Out of service, leaving the air	10-39	Your message delivered
10-8	In service, subject to call	10-40	Please tune to channel
10-9	Repeat message	10-42	Traffic accident at ...
10-10	Transmission completed	10-43	Traffic tie-up at ...
10-11	Talking too quickly	10-44	I have a message for you
10-12	Visitors present	10-45	All units within
10-13	Advise weather/road condition		range please report
10-16	Make pickup at	10-50	Emergency traffic at
10-17	Urgent business		this station (accident)
10-18	Anything for us?	10-60	What is next message
10-19	Nothing for you, return	10-62	Unable to copy, use
10-20	My location is		phone
10-21	Call by telephone	10-67	All units comply
10-22	Report in person to ...	10-70	Fire at ...
10-23	Stand by	10-71	Proceed with
10-24	Completed last assignment		transmission
10-25	Can you contact ....?	10-73	Speed trap at ...
10-26	Disregard last information	10-75	You are causing
10-27	I am moving to channel ...		interference
10-28	Identify your station	10-77	Negative contact
10-29	Time is up for contact	10-84	My telephone # is....
10-32	I will give you a radio check	10-85	My address is ....
		10-92	Talk closer to mike
		10-200	Police needed at ...

Communication Devices

Ham radio operators are legion. There are literally thousands of them all around the earth and they communicate with one another frequently. There are even community Ham radio clubs and networks who have set up emergency communication systems, even in foreign countries. To learn to use and have a license to be able to communicate, by radio the world over is a way to keep in touch of loved ones in far reaches of the globe

Communication Devices

One other type of communication device is the satellite telephone. The phone itself is quite expensive to purchase and pricy to use. Prices in recent years have come way down however. There are satellite phones that may be rented as well, but during a disaster you would probably not be able to acquire one to rent, so purchasing is the best alternative if you have the funds to do so. One more thing about satellite radios. During war time, they might not be of any use, so alternative plans for communicating should be established.

Radio Communication Requirements

There are six kinds, or levels, of amateur license for operating a Ham radio. They vary in degree of knowledge required and **frequency privileges** granted. Higher-class licenses have more comprehensive examinations. In return for passing a more difficult exam you earn more frequency privileges (frequency space and modes of operation). The first step is either the Novice or Technician license. The FCC issues these "beginner's" licenses to those who demonstrate the ability to operate an Amateur Radio transmitter safely and in properly allowed frequencies (freq).

The classes of licenses are as follows:

Class	Morse Code Test	Written Exam	Privileges
Technician	None	Tech-theory & regs	Restricted freq
General	None	Gen-theory & regs	All, except those reserved for advanced & Amateur Extra
Amateur Extra	None	All lower exam Elements plus Extra-Class theory	All amateur privileges

This is what an Amateur Radio license looks like...

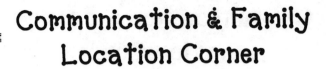

Communication & Family Location Corner

Morse Code

Flash lights can also be used for communication in the dark. However, those communicating in this manner must be able to understand some sort of signaling system. As a Boy Scout, I learned Morse Code and Semaphore (using flags). I can not remember any of the Semaphore signaling, but Morse Code, with a little re-tuning, I still remember.

Morse Code is a system of using what is called a telegraph key and an electronic signal transmitted over wire or by radio (or tapping on a tree trunk in the woods) or blinking a flash light off an on. The code is a series of dots and dashes. It isn't difficult and with a little study and practice it can be invaluable for communicating, provided the listener can also communicate in Morse Code. Just a bit of trivia: Morse Code was created by a man named Samuel B. Morse, fancy that! Below is the Morse Code chart.

Morse Code

Here are more charts below, pick the chart that is easiest to understand & learn a new skill.

A	.-	M	--	Y	-.--	6	-....
B	-...	N	-.	Z	--..	7	--...
C	-.-.	O	---	Ä	.-.-	8	---..
D	-..	P	.--.	Ö	---.	9	----.
E	.	Q	--.-	Ü	..--	.	.-.-.-
F	..-.	R	.-.	Ch	----	,	--..--
G	--.	S	...	0	-----	?	..--..
H	....	T	-	1	.----	!	..__.
I	..	U	..-	2	..---	:	---...
J	.---	V	...-	3	...--	"	.-..-.
K	-.-	W	.--	4	....-	'	.----.
L	.-..	X	-..-	5	.....	=	-..-

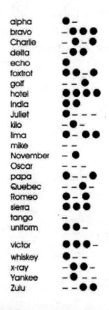

alpha
bravo
Charlie
delta
echo
foxtrot
golf
hotel
India
Juliet
kilo
lima
mike
November
Oscar
papa
Quebec
Romeo
sierra
tango
uniform

victor
whiskey
x-ray
Yankee
Zulu

one
two
tree
fo-war
fife
six
seven
eight
niner
zero

Communication & Family Location Corner

Morse Code

The three samples above are simple grids for Morse Code which may be used in any situation where Morse Code can be implemented. When using a flash light, a dash (-) is a longer flash while a dot (·) is a short flash. The Boy Scout flashlight is really handy for using Morse Code signaling. With just a little practice you will be able you to signal someone near or far.

Because your family may not be together when a disaster strikes, you will need to contact one another by whatever means you have at your disposal. It is strongly advised that you establish a relationship with another family or families to share and assist in making contact and communicate by delivering messages, providing a gathering point in case of disaster.

It is wise to instruct children to report to the same location when away from the home and this might be at a neighbor's or friend's house. When this is not possible, have the children gather at a fire station or police station in the area until they can locate all family members. In order to facilitate this important process, you will find on the next page a sample of a **Family Communications Plan.**

Communication & Family Location Corner

Family Location Plan

This should be kept by the main telephone in the home. Following this, you will find samples of **Cut-Out Cards** that should be kept in every family member's wallet or purse.

Ready
Prepare. Plan. Stay Informed.

Family Emergency Plan

Make sure your family has a plan in case of an emergency. Before an emergency happens, sit down together and decide how you will get in contact with each other, where you will go and what you will do in an emergency. Keep a copy of this plan in your emergency supply kit or another safe place where you can access it in the event of a disaster.

Out-of-Town Contact Name:	Telephone Number:
Email:	
Neighborhood Meeting Place:	Telephone Number:
Regional Meeting Place:	Telephone Number:
Evacuation Location:	Telephone Number:

Fill out the following information for each family member and keep it up to date.

Name:	Social Security Number:
Date of Birth:	Important Medical Information:
Name:	Social Security Number:
Date of Birth:	Important Medical Information:
Name:	Social Security Number:
Date of Birth:	Important Medical Information:
Name:	Social Security Number:
Date of Birth:	Important Medical Information:
Name:	Social Security Number:
Date of Birth:	Important Medical Information:
Name:	Social Security Number:
Date of Birth:	Important Medical Information:

Write down where your family spends the most time: work, school and other places you frequent. Schools, daycare providers, workplaces and apartment buildings should all have site-specific emergency plans that you and your family need to know about.

Work Location One	**School Location One**
Address:	Address:
Phone Number:	Phone Number:
Evacuation Location:	Evacuation Location:
Work Location Two	**School Location Two**
Address:	Address:
Phone Number:	Phone Number:
Evacuation Location:	Evacuation Location:
Work Location Three	**School Location Three**
Address:	Address:
Phone Number:	Phone Number:
Evacuation Location:	Evacuation Location:
Other place you frequent	**Other place you frequent**
Address:	Address:
Phone Number:	Phone Number:
Evacuation Location:	Evacuation Location:

Important Information	Name	Telephone Number	Policy Number
Doctor(s):			
Other:			
Pharmacist:			
Medical Insurance:			
Homeowners/Rental Insurance:			
Veterinarian/Kennel (for pets):			

Dial 911 for Emergencies

Communication & Family Location Corner

Family Location Plan

These printable cards can be found online through the Homeland Security website: www.ready.gov/america/makeaplan

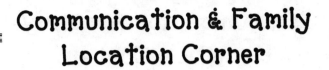

Ready
Prepare. Plan. Stay Informed.

Family Emergency Plan

Make sure your family has a plan in case of an emergency. Fill out these cards and give one to each member of your family to make sure they know who to call and where to meet in case of an emergency.

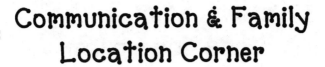

Communication & Family Location Corner

Family Location Plan

Following this, you will find samples of **Cut-Out Cards** that should be kept in every family member's wallet or purse.. You can find this particular cut-out card on the Red Cross website: www.redcross.org/prepare/eccard.pdf. They are in bright red and after cutting out as many as needed, fill them out and get them laminated for each family member.

**American Red Cross
Emergency Contact Card**

Directions:

1. Print this card for each household member.

2. Cut out the card along the dotted lines.

3. Write in the contact information for each household member, such as work, school and cell phone numbers. If you need additional space, use the back side of the card.

3. Fold the card so it fits in your pocket, wallet or purse.

4. Carry your card with you so it is available in the event of a disaster or other emergency when you will want to contact each other.

For more information on creating a family disaster plan and a disaster supplies kit, as well as other valuable disaster preparedness information, visit
www.redcross.org.

4/2005

Communication & Family Location Corner

Maintaining Communication

Once you are satisfied all family members are safe, or are being taken care of, maintaining communication with relief agencies or rescue teams and government is important. Usually, a battery or crank radio will allow you to listen to what's happening around you in your community. As a modern society, we have become so accustomed to readily available electricity, we tend to forget that battery powered communication devices should be a part of any communication plan. Store enough batteries to last a minimum of three days and longer if possible.

The American Red Cross has emergency communication services for military personnel to keep in touch with family in case of something important happening at home. For active duty personnel and their families, the phone number to contact the Red Cross is 877-272-7337.

Search & Rescue Resources

As an Eagle Scout, I had to learn the types of communication (called signaling in Scouting) mentioned in this **Corner.** When people cannot or are not able to communicate verbally, it becomes necessary to use other forms of communication. I could get very creative and talk about smoke signals, using drums, learning semaphore (flags) and such, but most people will not take the time or think it too difficult to learn. However, the use of a radio to communicate in times of urgency is probably the best method. Yes, a little more expensive than smoke or drum signals, but easier to use. The most difficult part with using radios, especially ham radios, is the testing and licensing aspect. As mentioned above, there are a few radios that may be used without licensing, but they have restricted range and use.

In locating family members during and after a disaster, all family members should participate in and be informed of, the family plan for locating one another and communicating each other's status. This will relieve stress and worry and then, the family can get on to surviving and recovering from the disaster.

In recent years, the American people have been urged to "get ready" and to prepare for emergencies – from natural disasters to terrorist attacks. But no one has ever given the public a simple, comprehensive and consistent tool to actually measure how prepared they really are. No one has ever provided individuals, communities, and the nation as a whole with practical "gauge" to assess their preparedness, recognize their successes and identify gaps where more work needs to be done. This is called your RQ (Readiness Quotient).

Two of the questions asked in the RQ test is: "In the last year, have you made a specific plan for how you and your family would communicate in an emergency situation if you were separated." AND "In the last year, have you established a specific meeting place to reunite in the event you and your family cannot return home or are evacuated?"

Communication & Family Location Corner

Search & Rescue Resources

In a national survey, only 44.1% of those responding said they had established some sort of communication plan with their family members. From power outages to terrorist attacks and war … hurricanes or tornados … floods to fires … earthquakes to manmade events … the most important message is simple: Be Prepared (The Boy Scout Motto). Get Ready. Be Informed.

There are some simple and effective means of communication when all family members are aware of them. I've named just a few below, to kick your brain into gear:

- Leave messages at friends or neighbors' if you can communicate with them
- Leave written messages in specified locations, known by all family members
- Flare guns shot up into the sky at certain time intervals, day or night
- Flash flares (those used for traffic incidents) set in certain locations
- Signal fire set in a certain location at a specified time
- Yes, making a certain sound, like beating a tree with a large stick with certain predetermined signal, such as SOS … three short raps on the tree followed by three long raps, ended with three short raps
- Use a whistle and breaking a light stick and waving it back and forth while whistling
- Use a compressed (hand held) air horn, like the ones used at sporting events by fans in the viewing stands.
- And last, but not least (maybe humorous) a trumpet or bugle

Communication & Family Location Corner

Search & Rescue Resources

A predetermined meeting place away from your home will save time and minimize confusion if your home is affected or your neighborhood is evacuated. Therefore, the above mentioned methods of signaling are really only beneficial if the family is in a reasonably close proximity of one another. That's why I keep harping on acquiring hand held radios of some sort and keeping them handy at all times. Better to have them and not need them and need them...............well, you know the rest.

Have you decided on a meeting place? Does everyone in your family know where it is? Be sure to update the location from time to time as circumstances require it i.e., not possible to meet there, neighbor/friend has moved. Always wise to have an alternate place in case the primary location is not adequate based on events and circumstances which may affect it.

Be sure to include your pets in your plan. Also be aware that pets are not permitted in emergency family shelters and some hotels will not accept them. (See Kiddie & Pet Corner for more information). Now that you have the plan in place, hold a drill/practice gathering at a predetermined location after work or school or an outing.

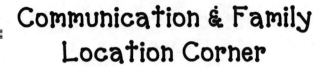

Communication & Family Location Corner

Search & Rescue Resources

Store vital information in the next of kin registry now – before the need arises. You can go to www.nokr.org and register your family/next of kin. Here are just a few scenarios where your information will be useful:

- · Missing or injured child, adult or senior
- · Lost child
- · Those suffering from Dementia or Alzheimer's
- · Accidents while traveling Nationally or Internationally
- · Unconscious person unable to communicate
- · Natural disasters (Hurricanes, Earthquakes, Tornados, Tsunamis, Fires)
- · Terrorist Acts Nationally or Internationally
- · Deceased person used to locate a next of kin or point of contact

Many people think that if they are carrying a driver's license, identification card or credit cards, authorities will know who their emergency contact is. These forms of identity only indicate who you are, not who should be contacted in the event of urgent need. To add to this problem, often times your current identification is not updated or readily available and it becomes very difficult and complex to locate emergency contacts. Who will speak for you or your family member when they can't? NOKR is a solution. This is very invaluable in case disaster strikes while out of the country. NOKR is the only organization which is global that provides a free emergency contact resource of this kind, to both citizens and emergency agencies.

All you have to do to request an emergency search is to contact your local Law Enforcement Agency. Below is a short list of Agencies, States, Countries and Organizations using or linking the free NOKR resource:

Communication & Family Location Corner

Search & Rescue Resources

USA.gov, the official U.S. gateway to all government information
Canadian Resource Centre for Victims of Crime (CRCVC)
United States Department of Agriculture (Tropical Storm and Hurricane Information)
United States Department of Homeland Security Disasterhelp.gov (Non-Government Orgs)
United States Department of Interior National Park Service United States Park Police
International Association of Coroners and Medical Examiners
United States Department of Defense (America Supports You)
United States Air Force Personnel Center Randolph AFB
International Committee of the Red Cross (ICRC)
International Atomic Energy Agency (IAEA)
American Red Cross (ARC)
United States Department Of State
Army National Guard Bureau
Guam Homeland Security
FEMA DMORT IV
United States Marine Corp
Also, 45 states and the District of Columbia

➤ Some discussion amongst family members should be directed to:
➤ Discuss what to do if a family member is injured or ill.
➤ Discuss what to do in the rare circumstance that authorities advise you to shelter-in-place.
➤ Discuss what to do if authorities advise you to evacuate.[link – to come]
➤ Plan where you would take your pets if you had to go to a public shelter where they are not permitted. Many communities are developing emergency animal shelters similar to shelters for people. Contact your local emergency management agency to find out about emergency animal shelters in your community, in the event that you have nowhere else to go and need to go to public shelter with your animals.

Communication & Family Location Corner

Search & Rescue Resources

> ➤ Post emergency numbers (fire, police, ambulance, etc.) by telephones. You may not have time in an emergency to look up critical numbers.

Note: You can adapt the Family Disaster Plan to any household—couples, related or unrelated individuals, adults without children, adults with children. Even people who live alone should create a Disaster Plan.

Practice Or Drill On What To Do In An Emergency

The old saying is true: Practice makes perfect. And although no one can ever be perfectly prepared... practicing or performing emergency drills is very important. Most schools require all students to participate in fire drills... every family should have emergency drills as well. Look for ways to make emergency drills and enjoyable family activity and avoid scaring your children or making them worry unnecessarily. An excellent resource for information on how to prepare children for emergencies is the FEMA web site.

Each family member, to whatever extent possible, should have easy access to, or have with them in their work place, automobile and/or home, an emergency 72 hour kit. This is especially important if/when family members are forced to be separated for a few days before being able to establish contact with other family members. See **Back To Basics Corner** for more detail.

72 hour kits come in all varieties, content and cost. Pick one that suites your needs best.

Communication & Family Location Corner

Search & Rescue Resources

It has been mentioned above, but to reiterate an important aspect of communication and family locating during and following a disaster is to learn some basic skills because once the family and loved ones are located, they may be injured and need care. Emergency services will be overwhelmed and hard pressed to give you and your family emergency service.

First aid training gives you competence and confidence to respond in an emergency situation with skills that can save a life; yours and your family's. Red Cross training offers complete, flexible programs that help you, your family and your community stay prepared for virtually any life-threatening situation.

If you haven't taken a first aid class in the past five years, it's time to do it! Training includes:

- CPR
- First Aid
- How to use an automated external defibrillator (AED)
- Injury prevention courses
- Blood borne pathogens training
- Community disaster education.

Contact your local Red Cross chapter for more information.

Communication & Family Location Corner

LOCATING FAMILY LOST OR SEPARATED IN THE WILDERNESS by AIR

This final section will deal with other essential search and rescue elements if someone is lost in remote areas and having nothing necessarily to do with a disaster or emergency, other than being lost. Much of what has been discussed above may also be used by the person who is lost and the person or persons doing the searching. This section will give some basic instruction to the person being searched for because generally speaking, those doing the searching will be professional search and rescue teams and will understand signaling from the air.

The Civil Air patrol is an auxiliary of the United States Air Force and participates in a great number of searches for lost people, downed aircraft etc. It might be suggested that some basic signaling skills for communicating with aircraft from the ground be learned. The Civil Air Patrol pilots, and those riding with them to assist in the searching, know and understand ground signals. Having a hand held radio will, of course, be the best way to communicate with an airplane and other searchers, but you might find yourself lost without a radio or........your batteries are dead. Some simple rules to follow for signaling from the ground are: 1) Use contrasting colors ie., red, orange, yellow. 2) Signals should be 10-12 feet long and 3-4 feet wide. The larger the better. 3) Place in an open area. Signal fires may also be used and is sometimes the only way to signal if a large, open area cannot be located, taking care not to start a forest fire. Once the fire has started and is burning good, find some moss or green (not dry) wood with leaves etc. to burn because this generates more smoke, making the fire easier to see from the air.

Following are some basic and simple ground to air/air to ground signals from the Civil Air Patrol:

Communication & Family Location Corner

Ground to Air/Air to Ground Signals

1. REQUIRE ASSISTANCE	V
2. REQUIRE MEDICAL ASSISTANCE	X
3. NO or NEGATIVE	N
4. YES or AFFIRMATIVE	Y
5. PROCEEDING IN THIS DIRECTION	↑

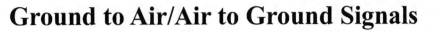

NEED MEDICAL ASSISTANCE URGENT USED ONLY WHEN LIFE IS AT STAKE	ALL OK DO NOT WAIT	CAN PROCEED SHORTLY WAIT IF PRACTICAL
LIE SUPINE	WAVE ONE ARM OVERHEAD	ONE ARM HORIZONTAL
NEED MECHANICAL HELP OR PARTS LONG DELAY	DO NOT ATTEMPT TO LAND HERE	LAND HERE
BOTH ARMS HORIZONTAL	BOTH ARMS WAVE ACROSS FACE	BOTH ARMS FORWARD HORIZONTALLY SQUATTING AND POINTING IN DIRECTION OF LANDING
USE MESSAGE DROP	OUR RECEIVER IS OPERATING	NEGATIVE (NO)
MAKE THROWING MOTION	CUP HANDS OVERHEAD	CLOTH WAVED HORIZONTALLY
AFFIRMATIVE (YES)		PICK US UP PLANE ABANDONED
CLOTH WAVED VERTICALLY		BOTH ARMS VERTICAL

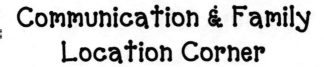

Communication & Family Location Corner

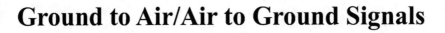

Ground to Air/Air to Ground Signals

Understanding what the pilot/airplane is trying to tell you, even after he has seen your ground signals or fire, is also important. Following are some basic AND SIMPLE means for understanding the aircraft's signals:

· When signaling you, the aircraft will:

- Generally travel at under 100 mph
- Maneuver with all external lights on (even during daylight)
- Rotating tail beacon (if available)
- Landing lights
- Taxi lights

So, remember: **Lights on = Signaling   Light off= Normal flying**

OTHER SIGNALS

- Strobe lights (usually not something a hiker or hunter carries), or a flashlight is very useful in signally aircraft at night
- Signal mirror. Can be purchased in most sporting goods stores
- Space blanket also can serve as a reflector/large signal mirror
- Shadows
  Pile rocks, brush or snow
  Scrape or tramp out trenches in dirt, sand or snow
- Smoke signal flares (again, not something usually carried while hunting or hiking
- Aerial Flares or flare gun (more likely to be carried)

A signal mirror is small, light and easily carried in a backpack. True signaling mirrors have a hole in the middle to look

Communication & Family Location Corner

Ground to Air/Air to Ground Signals

through while signaling, enabling you to target a particular spot or area. If trying to get attention from anyone who might be looking, sweep the horizon slowly – flashes can be seen for miles.

An aircraft may attempt to signal someone on the ground by certain movements of the plane. Below are pictures of basic movements of "yes," "no," "message received and understood" and "message received but not understood.":

Leaving signs on the ground to communicate with searchers is also an important element of communicating. Locating and finding family members if caught in a situation of having been separated by long distances due to disaster and having to find your way back home and perhaps getting off course (lost). Gleaning from my old Boy Scout manual, I have included some simple ground signs/signals to assist searchers and the lost soul.

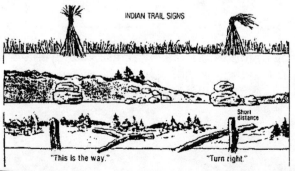

INDIAN TRAIL SIGNS

"This is the way."   "Turn right."

Scout Trail Signs

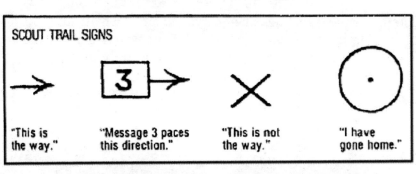

SCOUT TRAIL SIGNS

"This is the way."

"Message 3 paces this direction."

"This is not the way."

"I have gone home."

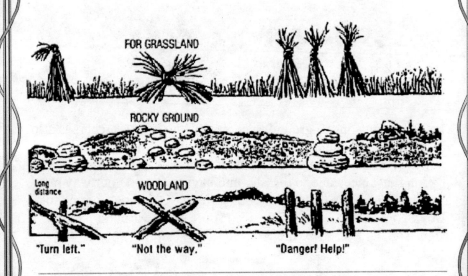

FOR GRASSLAND

ROCKY GROUND

Long distance

WOODLAND

"Turn left."

"Not the way."

"Danger! Help!"

When making or following trail signs, use your eyes and take it easy. Be sure that the sign you see or make is actually a sign that is recognized as such. may be found in most sporting goods stores.

Finding Your Way

One last suggestion for assisting in locating someone who is lost, and of course important for the person who IS lost, is to have a compass. Compasses are small, light and easily read without too much difficulty. Again, all types of compasses may be found in most sporting goods stores.

Compasses can range in price from just a few dollars, to over $100.00. They can be very small as well and fit nicely into a pocket. Compasses can be give false readings if used in the vicinity of magnetic items or large amounts of metal.

If you are lost, standing in the middle of nowhere, and you have no idea where to go or how to get there, and you don't have a compass, there are some other simple ways to find compass directions by using the sun and stars. More on this topic will be discussed in the **Outdoor Survival Corner.**

If you have an analog wrist watch (one with hands that move), you can use the time to find north. Hold your watch up in front of you, and let the short hand that indicates the hour point at the sun. While holding it like this, cut the angle between the hour hand and 12 o'clock in two, (*noonwards* if the time is before 6am or after 6pm), that way is south. (The reason you have to cut the angle in two/half, is because the clock takes two rotations while the sun takes only one around the earth, actually it is the sun rotating around the earth, but never mind).

Communication & Family Location Corner

Finding Your Way

If you are wearing a digital watch, draw an analog watch on a piece of paper, or scratch one in the dirt with a stick. Then, mark the hour hand by using the digital watch time. The rest of the method is identical.

This method may be used even when it is cloudy. Although you may not be able to see the sun, it may still cast a shadow. If you take a small stick and push it into the dirt you may see its shadow. You just have to remember that the shadow points the opposite way from the sun, but the rest of it is quite similar to above.

To make a simple, but effective compass, you will need a needle or piece of metal of the same size. If careful, a small paper clip with one of its angles being bent straight will work. You will need something to hold some water. A needle can in fact float on the water, that is, on the surface tension forces if placed carefully on the surface (same with the paper clip). Just place it carefully down on the surface of the water. This demands a lot of patience and a steady hand. Breaking the water tension will cause the needle to sink. A couple of tricks is to place the needle on a piece of paper and place the paper on the surface. If the paper floats, no problem, it will work the same and if it sinks, the needle will remain on the surface ... usually. Use a fork to lower the needle onto the water, or rubbing the needle in your hair to "grease" it up a bit will help it to float. If the needle is magnetic (to magnetize it you can scratch the tip or head on a rock vigorously for several seconds) it will work as a regular compass and will lay north and south. Which end is north, you ask? Well, I'm afraid you'll have to use some other hints to help, such as moss on the north sides of the trees, the sun, the stars and aunts normally like to build their nests on the south side of trees/hills/banks etc.

Communication & Family Location Corner

Finding Your Way

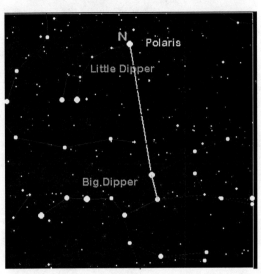

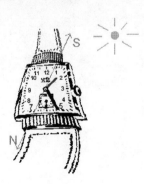

Hopefully you will be able to use some of these helpful hints in locating and communicating with family members during disasters or finding them if lost. Communicating with emergency assist agencies is critical as well, but we must all know how to be self-reliant and learn some basic skills to help ourselves and our family and friends in time of crisis. I hope you have found this **Corner** helpful.

Kiddie/Pet Safety Corner

☂☂☂ Kiddie & Pet Safety Corner ☂☂☂

Simple steps to help you in this corner:

1. Understanding how children cope during a disaster

2. Do your children know what to do during a disaster?

3. Teaching children important emergency symbols

4. Communicate with your children

5. Ready for an emergency "Game"

6. Prepare a youth emergency back pack kit

7. Prepare a baby emergency kit

8. Prepare a pet emergency kit

9. Taking care of pets in a disaster

10. Keep it simple, don't get overwhelmed & have FUN!

♂♂♂ Kiddie & Pet Safety Corner ♂♂♂

Children Need Help Coping With A Disaster

Natural disasters may cause stress for people of all ages, but adults need to realize children may need extra help in coping with any disaster.

A child's reaction to a disaster will vary depending on age, maturity, and previous experience. Many children express common fears during or after a disaster: darkness, abandonment, and death. Children have trouble understanding what the disaster is and why it happens. Try to understand what is causing anxieties and fears. Be aware that following a disaster, children are most afraid of the following:

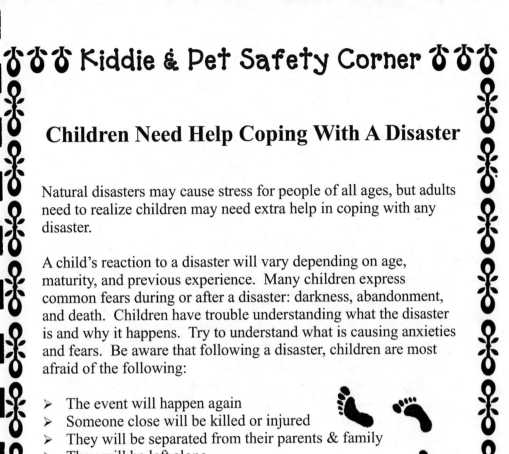

- ➢ The event will happen again
- ➢ Someone close will be killed or injured
- ➢ They will be separated from their parents & family
- ➢ They will be left alone
- ➢ Being exposed to television news
- ➢ Feeling a loss of control
- ➢ Being anxious
- ➢ Being exposed to others' stories of trauma or disaster

When children experience a natural disaster, parents and other adults should encourage them to express their feelings. Children usually take their lead in a situation by reading the emotions of adults. Adults should share their true feelings about the incident, but maintain a sense of calm for the child's sense of well-being. If a young child is asking questions about the event, answer them simply without the elaboration needed for an older child or adult. If a child has difficulty expressing feelings, allow the child to draw a picture or tell a story of what happened through their own eyes.

Children may feel at fault for the disaster. Parents should reassure them that they are not responsible for what occurred. They may also feel abandoned or neglected by parents who are busy cleaning

Children Need Help Coping With A Disaster

and rebuilding after the disaster. Close contact assures these children that you are there for them and will not abandon them.

Spending extra time putting children to bed at night can help ease their concerns. Everybody loves a story, and if you begin with "Once upon a time..." you'll have their immediate attention. Stories can be short and have a particular character that you use night after night. For instance, you could use a Frisbee, that had a different tail each night, or you could use a small pig named "Pee Wee Pickle Bum" who got in all sorts of mischief. You can tell stories of when you were a small child and what your fears were, or you could tell funny stories about a made up boy named "Tom" or inspirational stories and on and on and on. The important thing is the time spent with your children.

Other unusual behaviors a child may exhibit include hitting and kicking in anger or frustration, becoming quiet and withdrawn, retreating to behaviors shown at a younger age, exhibiting symptoms of illness, or refusing to be out of a parent's sight.

When children exhibit such behaviors, they are craving attention. Parents need to continually respond to their needs and repeatedly assure them they are loved and their feelings are important. Here are some ways in which to reassure your children:

> - Hug and touch your children
> - Calmly and firmly provide factual information about the recent disaster
> - Encourage your children to talk about their feelings; be honest about your own
> - Spend extra time with your children at bedtime
> - Re-establish a schedule for work, play meals & rest
> - Involve your children by giving them specific chores to help them feel they are helping to restore family and community life
> - Encourage your children to help develop a family disaster plan
> - Make sure your children know what to do when they hear smoke detectors, fire alarms, and local community warning systems such as horns or sirens
> - Praise and recognize responsible behavior
> - Understand that your children will need to mourn their own losses
> - Monitor and limit your children's exposure to the media
> - Use support networks, such as family members, friends, community organizations, faith-based institutions, or other resources that work for your family

☙☙☙ Kiddie & Pet Safety Corner ☙☙☙

Children Need Help Coping With A Disaster

Preparing for disaster helps everyone in the family accept the fact that disasters do happen, and it provides an opportunity to identify and collect the information needed for that preparation so that when people feel prepared, they cope better; so do their children.

Adults also need to remember several facts:

➢ Children do not have mature reasoning skills
➢ Children lack an accurate understanding of cause and effect
➢ Children have not had the chance to become skilled at handling stress
➢ Children need to discuss stress issues honestly and at their level of understanding
➢ Children need help to prevent pressures from building
➢ If the stress reaches a crisis level in the child, seek help from professional counselors.

Parents should be alerted to these signs that indicate your child may be feeling continued stress after a traumatic event and these symptoms could be called "Post-traumatic Stress"

➢ Refusal to return to school and clinging behavior
➢ Shadowing the mother or father around the house
➢ Sleep disturbances such as nightmares, screaming during sleep
➢ Bed wetting
➢ Have problems staying or falling asleep
➢ Loss of concentration and irritability
➢ Behavior problems, which are not typical for the child
➢ Physical complaints (Stomachache, headache, dizziness) for which a physical cause cannot be found
➢ Withdrawal from family and friends
➢ Decreased activity
➢ Preoccupation with the events
➢ Acting younger than their age

☂☂☂ Kiddie & Pet Safety Corner ☂☂☂

Children Need Help Coping With A Disaster

After a stressful or traumatic event, your child may react differently to normal or unexpected events. Some examples of traumatic events are:

- ➢ Being in a car crash
- ➢ Death of a family member
- ➢ Seeing violence in the home, the community, or on TV
- ➢ Being in a natural disaster such as a fire
- ➢ Being in a disaster caused by others such as terrorists

The care of a child goes beyond the initial reaction or the physical injuries in a disaster situation. Your child & family members are emotionally affected by the events when the disaster happens and for some time afterwards. The reactions to the stress after a traumatic event are usually relatively brief for a child. It is difficult to predict how each child will react, however, when the reaction will occur and how long it will last.

I hope this corner has given you some suggestions for helping children to cope with the effects of disaster, as well as how to be prepared before a disaster strikes.

One more comment:

Remember to learn about the emergency plans that are in place at your child's school, child care facility, or other places where your child stays when not with you. Contact the school principal's office, child care facility, or responsible adult to find out how evacuations and other emergency procedures will be handled while your child is in their care. Also, make sure to always keep up-to-date emergency contact information on file at the school or with the adult caring for your children.

Get Ready, Get Set, Get Prepared!

Do You Know What To Do In An Emergency?

An emergency is a time when you need help from a police officer, firefighter, or doctor. Take these steps to make sure you're prepared:

- Know you full name, parents' full names address (including city & state), and phone number (including area code).
- Memorize your parents' work and cell phone numbers
- Ask your parents to post a list of emergency numbers you may need to keep by the phone
- With an adult, talk about different times you may need help and what you should do
- With your parents, pick a safe place you can go to near your house if you need help right away
- Have a fire drill with your parents and family members so you know what to do in case of a fire

If there's an emergency:

- Go to a safe place, right away
- Call 911 or dial 0. (Ask an adult which is best.) Remember you can call both for free from a pay phone
- The operator will ask you what the emergency is, your name, full address, and phone number

Teaching Children Important Symbols

Teach children how and when to call for help.
They should call 9-1-1 if you live in a 9-1-1
service area. If not, check the telephone
directory for local emergency numbers and
place the numbers near the telephone,
clearly visible to children. Even very young
children can learn how and when to call for
emergency assistance.

If your child can read numbers but not words,
the symbols on this page may help a child
to find the right number to call.

As you explain each picture, have your
child point it out to you and use the information
below to help them know important
information.

MY FAMILY NAME: _____

MY PHONE NUMBER: _____

MY ADDRESS: _____

MY TOWN: _____

MY COUNTY: _____

MY MOM and DAD'S NAMES:

_____

_____

AMBULANCE

FIRE

POLICE/SHERIFF

RED CROSS

PARENTS

☿☿☿ Kiddie & Pet Safety Corner ☿☿☿

Communicate With Your Kids!

C Create a family communication plan so you can get in tough with family members. **(See Communication and Family Location Corner)** Give copies of contact information and meeting locations to everyone in your family

O Options are available: telephones, cell phones, and e-mail are all great ways to get in touch with family members

M Make sure you know the emergency plan at your children's school

M Make a decision about where you will meet in case you can't get home during an emergency

U Understand that it may take time to get through to everyone. Try to be patient

N Needs of your pets should be kept in mind. Keep a pet carrier for easy transport

I Inform yourself, watch news broadcasts, read online news updates, or listen to a battery-operated or crank radio for official guidance during an emergency, remember, preparing in advance adds comfort

C Copies of your family emergency plan should be in your emergency supply kit in case you need to leave in a hurry

A Ask kids to discuss their concerns and feelings; do they understand the family plan?

T Take the kids to visit the "meeting spots" so that they are familiar and feel comfortable finding them on their own if necessary

E Emergencies take many forms; categorize different types of emergencies and discuss the level of concern related to each one

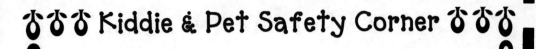

Ready For An Emergency Game

Here is a fun game to teach your children what to do in an emergency. This game came by way of the Random Sampler from Alison Affeltranger; this game can be very helpful in learning more about how to take better care of your home during a crisis.

Get Ready:
Divide family members into teams of two, pairing one parent or older child with each younger child. Select team colors; place a colored sticker dot for each team in various places (see below). Prepare a game sheet with different questions for each team.

Get Set:
Gather the family. Assign each member to a team and a color, and give each team a game sheet.

Go!
Each team searches for its own colored dots and places them on the game sheet, then answers the questions. The first team that answers correctly wins a prize.

Dot placement and questions:

Water: Where is the main turn-off valve to the house?
How do you turn it off?
Where do you turn off a toilet's water supply?

Electricity: Where is the main breaker to turn off power to the house?
Where are the circuit breakers or fuse box located?
How do you reset a tripped breaker or replace a blown fuse?

Gas: How do you turn off the supply to the main house?
The water heater?
The furnace?

Smoke Alarms: Where are the smoke alarms?
How many do we have?
Do they require batteries that need to be changed regularly?

Telephone: Who do we call in an emergency?
How can we contract Mom or Dad?
When might we appropriately dial 9-1-1 (or our emergency number)?

Evacuation: Where should we meet if we have to leave the house during an emergency?

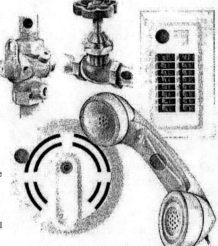

☘☘☘ Kiddie & Pet Safety Corner ☘☘☘

Youth Emergency Back Pack Kit

Place back pack underneath head of bed with handle facing out for a quick grab. Easier said than done, keep an extra pair of hard sole shoes near your child's bed for quick evacuation, especially if it is in the middle of the night. Items to include are as follows:

- 1 back pack (or a tote bag, duffle bag or sm suit case on wheels)
- 1 warm jacket or sweater and pair of gloves
- 1 sweat shirt and 1 sweat pants
- 2 pair of socks
- change of under garments
- small blanket or emergency blanket (mylar, space, fleece)
- coloring books and crayons or writing pads with pencils
- reading books
- small stuffed animal for security as a stress relief
- flashlight with extra batteries or light sticks
- 1 emergency poncho
- 1 hand/body warmer (2 per packet)
- toothbrush/toothpaste (trial size)
- lotion (trial size)
- shampoo/conditioner (trail size)
- 4 moist hand towelettes, wash cloth/hand towel
- 4 sterile alcohol swabs to clean wounds or cuts
- variety pack of Band-aids
- 2 pocket size facial tissue packs
- bar of soap or hand sanitizer
- nail file or nail clippers (optional)
- tweezers, sm pair of scissors (optional)
- 1 blow whistle
- 1 small compass
- mess kit for meals
- 3-day supply of food (see Back to Basics Corner)

Zip Lock Bag Items For Back Pack Kit

☗☗☗ Kiddie & Pet Safety Corner ☗☗☗

 # Baby Emergency Kit

The easiest way to keep an emergency kit for your baby is to keep the baby diaper bag filled at all times and always keep next to the crib, so at a moments notice you can grab the bag and run. The items you will most likely need to keep in this bag are as follows:

- ➤ (1) baby bottle
- ➤ (2) bottles of water
- ➤ Single packets of formula, juice
- ➤ Diapers - as many as you can stuff in
- ➤ Packet of baby wipes
- ➤ Baby food jars with spoon
- ➤ Baby bibs
- ➤ Baby pacifier, sippie cup
- ➤ T-shirts, gown, beanie, sleepers, booties, burp cloth
- ➤ Powder, lotion, ointment, oil
- ➤ Q-tips
- ➤ Blankets (soft cotton or fleece)
- ➤ Baby toys - small
- ➤ Thermometer
- ➤ Ear/nose bulb
- ➤ Medicine dropper & medications
- ➤ Clothing, depending on what time of year
- ➤ Snack foods - crackers, cheerios, etc.
- ➤ Safety pins
- ➤ Wash clothes, small towel & soap

Pet Emergency Kit

If you are a pet owner, your family disaster plan must include your pets. In the event of a disaster, if you must evacuate, the most important thing you can do to protect your pets is to evacuate them, too. Leaving pets behind, even if you try to create a safe place for them, is likely to result in their being injured, lost, or worse. So prepare now for the day when you and your pets may have to leave your home. Things that should be included are as follows:

- Pet food & treats - 3-day supply
- Drinkable water in plastic bottles and dish - 3 day supply
- Can opener for canned food & disposable utensils
- Pet medications and medical records in a waterproof container, vet information (written down on paper)
- Sturdy leashes, harnesses and/or carriers or crates so you can move your pets safely and they can't escape (remember they may be scared and may act differently than usual), collar and pet tags.
- Current photos of your pet(s) in case they get lost
- Pet beds, toys (tennis ball, frisbee, etc) if you have room
- Sanitation items such as poop bags, pooper scooper, litter box, litter
- Blankets, paper towels, grooming supplies
- Pet first aid kit (see contents below)

The items listed below can be added to your First aid kit or make up a pet first aid kit:

- 3-day supply of any medications or vitamins your pet normally takes
- Name, address and phone # of vet
- Tape
- Scissors
- Antibacterial soap
- Cotton balls/gauze
- Hydrogen peroxide
- Pet first aid manual

✿✿✿ Kiddie & Pet Safety Corner ✿✿✿

 ## Taking Care of Pets

If you need to evacuate (leave your home for safer ground) take your pet(s) with you. Leaving pets behind, even if you try to create a safe place for them, is not the best action. However, pets cannot go to emergency shelters where people are, unless they are service animals, like dogs for the visually impaired. They may affect the health and safety of other occupants. If this is a scenario that could happen, you need to plan ahead and keep the information together in your family emergency or pet kit on what you have decided.

Here are some items you should consider:

How much food will you need?   _____
What kind of food?   _____
What type of carrier is needed?   _____
ID Tag Numbers   _____
Shot types & dates   _____
                                             _____
Veterinarian information   _____

Find out what your community's plans and resources are for protecting pets in an emergency. The following ideas can help as resources for planning to ensure your pet's safety before an emergency happens:

Contact hotels, motels, friends, relatives and kennels outside your immediate area to know in advance where you will shelter your pet(s).

If you have more than one pet, they may be more comfortable if they are kept together, but in an emergency that might not be possible.

If you are under a disaster warning, keep your pets inside with you so you don't have to look for them if you have to evacuate.

👣👣👣 Kiddie & Pet Safety Corner 👣👣👣

 ## Taking Care of Pets

Make sure they are wearing collars and identification tags.

Relying on a neighbor or friend if you get trapped away from home due to a disaster or other emergency, will be better for your pet if you have already made arrangements for them to step in and take care of the pet in an emergency. The temporary caretaker should have a phone number to reach you and all the instructions necessary to properly care for the animal. Those instructions should include a signed authorization for veterinary care and financial limits for that care.

There are many agencies that have information regarding your pets. They are listed below:

American Red Cross
American Veterinary Medical Association (AVMA)
Emergency Animal Rescue Service (EARS)
Federal Emergency Management Agency (FEMA)
Local animal shelters
The Humane Society
National Animal Poison Control
Pet Travel and Lodging Resources
American Kennel Club
American Society for the Prevention of Cruelty to Animals
(ASPCA)

Much of the information researched for this corner came from many resources including fema.gov, The American Red Cross web site, The US Department of Homeland Security web site, The American Kennel Club, fda.gov, Weber County Emergency Management (CERT) publications, The Department of Public Safety web site, Random Sampler and www.mcgruff.org

Disaster-Specific
Preparedness Corner

Disaster-Specific
Preparedness Corner

Simple steps to help you with this corner

1. Know that each disaster has specific aspects and preparation is needed for each

2. Learn that flooding occurs even in arid locations; search out evacuation routes for your area; keep safe food and water supply for at least three days on hand

3. Purchase and learn to use emergency radios; keep emergency kits handy; prepare your home if you have to evacuate

4. Understand where tornadoes and hurricanes are most likely to hit; prepare a safe room or underground storm cellar

5. Understand terms used by emergency services to understand specific disasters

6. Take precautions when out of doors during lightening storms; learn how to protect yourself if in or out of doors during an earthquake

7. Protect against extreme weather conditions ie., extreme cold, heavy snow and extreme heat; learn basic precautions against frost bite and hypothermia

8. If stranded in a vehicle in a snow storm, stay put and wait for emergency help; understand that an emergency kit with warm clothing should be kept in your vehicle

9. Eat often and keep hydrated during cold and hot weather; don't travel alone in a winter storm or in extreme heat

10. Keep it simple, don't get overwhelmed and have FUN!

Disaster-Specific Preparedness Corner

This **Corner** is to instruct you in taking actions before, during and after an event that are unique to each disaster.

Natural disasters such as floods, hurricanes, tornadoes, earthquakes & fires affect thousands of people every year in virtually every corner of the globe. We need to know what our exposure to harm from these disasters is and take precautions to protect ourselves, our families and our communities. Most of this book already provides information for preparing for emergencies. The difference in this **Corner** is that, because each disaster has its own unique components which require different types of preparation, we are being more specific in providing information for preparation and actions unique to each hazard.

FLOODS

Floods are the most common type of disaster in the United States. Floods can impact local communities, entire cities and towns and even regions. Fortunately, floods do not happen instantly, giving us time to "gear up" as it were, to the event. Usually we are warned of impending flooding and can gather up our emergency gear and get out of Dodge. There are floods, especially in the west, that are called flash floods and do come almost instantly, hence the name "flash flood." And, flash floods may happen a long distance from where it is raining.

Flash floods usually can be heard before seen and are extremely dangerous because they carry boulders, buildings and other large debris because of their high speed of travel and will carry away most anything in its path. If caught in a flash flood, even in a vehicle, you will be swept miles away and/or killed by this debris, if not drowned first. If a levee or dam breaks, the flooding will have many similarities to a flash flood and downstream from the levee or dam may have very little or no warning. Take for example the Teton Dam disaster in 1976.

Disaster-Specific Preparedness Corner

Very little warning was given to the people in Rexburg, Idaho and they left with nothing. So, a word of caution: **Be aware of flood hazards, no matter where you live!** Especially if you live in a low lying area, near rivers or downstream from a dam. An earthquake of sufficient strength can cause a dam to give way; now you have a dual problem … an earthquake and a flood for which you have to deal. Even small streams have potentials for flooding. Take for example the flooding in St. George, Utah in 2005. The Virgin River, (most of the time a very small stream with very little water), suddenly turned into a raging torrent from rains upstream. The residents who built their luxurious homes next to the river never in a million years thought this tiny stream would turn into a mighty river, tearing their precious homes from off their foundations and carrying them miles downstream.

Disaster-Specific
Preparedness Corner

Ask yourself the following questions:

· Am I at risk for flooding if I live in a desert state with bare hills, deep canyons, and dry land?
· Is there a need to have a flood disaster plan and a disaster supplies kit?
· Should I consider purchasing flood insurance for my home and property?

Of course, the answer to all three questions is "YES."

BEFORE THE FLOOD

To prepare for a flood you should:

· Avoid building or living in a flood plain, or downstream from a dam, unless you elevate your home and reinforce it
· Elevate your furnace, water heater and electrical panel
· Install "check valves or backwash prevention valves" in sewer

- Water from backing up into drains
- Construct barriers to prevent flood waters from entering the building
- Seal foundation walls in the basement from the outside to prevent seepage

DURING THE FLOOD

If a flood is eminent in your area you should:

- Listen to radio and TV for information and evacuation instructions
- Be aware that flash flooding may occur, even if the flood is slow in building in strength; move to higher ground immediately, not waiting for instructions
- Be aware of streams, drainage channels and irrigation ditches, canyons and other areas with or without such typical warnings as rain clouds or heavy rain

If you must prepare to evacuate, you should do the following:

- Secure your home. If you have time, bring outdoor furniture inside. Move essential items to an upper floor. Secure important documents from water damage and secure valuables.
- If possible, turn off utilities at the juncture where they come into the house ie., electrical and gas. Disconnect all electric appliances and do not touch anything electrical if wet or standing in water.

Disaster-Specific
Preparedness Corner

If you have to leave your home, remember these evacuation tips:

- **Do not walk through moving water.** Even six inches can make you lose your footing and fall down. If you have to walk in water, walk with a walking stick and walk near the shallowest end or where the water is not moving.

- **Do not drive into flooded areas or attempt to cross a flooded stream or wash.** If flood waters rise around your car while you are inside, abandon your car as quickly as possible and move to higher ground if you can do so safely. You and your vehicle can be swiftly carried away.

DRIVING FLOOD FACTS

The following are important points to remember when driving in flood conditions:

- Six inches of water will reach the bottom of most passenger cars causing loss of control and danger of stalling out; if in this much water, drive slowly so as not to splash water up on the engine
- A foot of water will float most passenger automobiles and pickup trucks
- Two feet of rushing water can carry away most vehicles including pickups and sport utility vehicles (SUV's)
- Never attempt to cross a stream, wash or even a dip in the road with rushing water in it; even if the water is not very deep because more water may be coming and catch you while attempting to cross

The following are guidelines for the period after the flood has subsided:

- Listen for news reports on radio (or TV if you have one available) to learn if the flood waters are subsiding and whether

Disaster-Specific Preparedness Corner

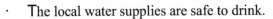

- The local water supplies are safe to drink.
- Avoid floodwaters; water may be contaminated with oil, gasoline, or raw sewage. Even dead animals and people. Water may also be electrically charged from downed or underground power lines.
- Again, avoid moving water, both by walking and vehicle
- Stay especially away from downed power lines, even if you are not in the water ie, in a boat or other vehicle; notify the power company if possible.
- Return home only when authorities indicate it is safe.
- Use extreme caution when entering buildings and your home; there may be hidden damage, particularly in foundations and upper floors or over basements.
- Service damaged septic tanks, cesspools, pits, and leaching systems as soon as possible by having them pumped. Damaged and leaking sewage systems are a serious health hazard.
- Clean and disinfect everything that got wet. Mud left from the floodwaters may be contaminated with sewage and/or chemicals.

There are disaster clean up services in most cities, but after a flood they will be overwhelmed with calls from thousands of others, so you must provide and fend for yourself after returning home.

Disaster-Specific
Preparedness Corner

This is why one should have, on hand, tall rubber boots, gloves (preferably rubber coated to keep chemicals off your skin) and face masks to protect against breathing chemicals and flat shovels to clear out the mud and debris that floods inevitable bring into buildings. You can minimize damage to your home by boarding up windows, putting sand bags in front of doors and ground level windows to keep as much mud and debris out of your home as possible.

ADDITIONAL INFORMATION

Consider the following facts:

- Flood losses are **not covered** by homeowners' insurance policies
- FEMA manages the National Flood Insurance Program, which makes federally-backed flood insurance available in towns and communities that agree to adopt and enforce flood plain management ordinances, so check where you live to see if your community is one that qualifies for FEMA's NFIP insurance.

Disaster-Specific Preparedness Corner

- Most insurance companies offer flood insurance. Check with yours to see if the company you have your homeowners' policy which offers coverage in your area.
- There is most always a moratorium for flood insurance coverage (even from your local insurance company) of 30 days before it takes effect, so don't go out and buy it when it starts to rain. Noah built his ark long before it began to rain.
- Flood insurance is normally available even if your home is in a flood-prone area. Keep in your possession a battery or crank operated NOAA (National Oceanic and Atmospheric Administration) radio, not just for floods, but other emergencies.

Disaster-Specific Preparedness Corner

TORNADOES

Tornadoes are nature's most violent storms. Spawned from powerful thunder storms, tornadoes can cause fatalities and devastate a town or community, in just seconds. A tornado appears as a rotating, funnel shaped cloud that extends from a large thunderhead (storm) to the ground with whirling winds that sometimes reach 300 mph. They move horizontally and their paths can be in excess of one mile wide and 50 miles long. Every state is some risk of a tornado, but there are areas of the United States where tornadoes are very much commonplace. The map below shows what is termed "Tornado Alley."

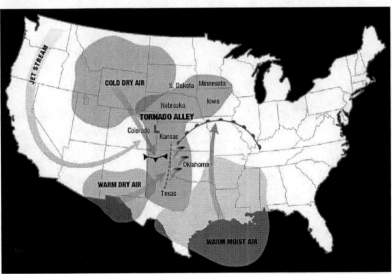

I'm probably preaching to the choir here, but for those who may be new residents of "Tornado Alley" I am going to share some vital information. Experienced tornado watchers may even find some of it informative. I'm keeping with the KISS method.

By now, everyone knows that Dorothy was handily removed from Kansas by a tornado and she and her dog Todo were whisked away to a land of OZ. Tornadoes are very powerful and would give King Kong a run for the money. They can lift people, animals, machinery and automobiles and displace them far away. Most tornadoes are clearly visible, but sometimes they are obscured by low lying clouds and rain. In many instances tornadoes will form almost instantly and develop so rapidly that many are caught unawares and little warning or advanced preparation can be made.

Before a tornado hits, the wind may become very still. A cloud of debris can give a tornado's location away even if the funnel is not visible. Tornadoes often are formed at the end of a storm system and right behind it you may see clear, sunlit skies.

 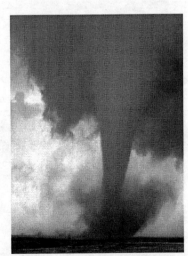

The following are facts about tornadoes:

· They may strike suddenly without any, or very little warning

Disaster-Specific
Preparedness Corner

- The may be invisible to the naked eye until they pick up dust or debris or until a cloud forms in the funnel
- Typically, a tornado moves from southwest to northeast, but they also move in all directions
- The average speed of a tornado horizontally over the ground is around 30 mph while they may be stationary, or even move at 70 mph
- Tornados may also follow hurricanes and tropical storms as they move inland
- Waterspouts are tornadoes that form over water; when one is observed and you are on the water, move to land as quickly as possible
- Tornadoes most frequently form east of the Rocky Mountains during the spring and summer months; we had a big one hit Salt Lake City in August of 1999, right in the middle of the Rocky Mountains

Disaster-Specific Preparedness Corner

- Peak tornado season in the southern states is March through May; in the northern states, it is late spring through early summer; the one in Salt Lake City was in August, go figure
- Tornadoes are most likely to form in the hottest part of the day, generally between 3:00pm and 9:00pm, but can occur any time
- Usually around dinner time and other most inconvenient times as well

KNOW THE TERMS

Familiarize yourself with these terms to help identify a tornado hazard:

TORNADO WATCH

Tornadoes are possible. Remain alert for approaching storms. Watch the sky and stay tuned to NOAA Weather Radio, commercial radio or TV

TORNADO WARNING

A tornado has been sighted or indicated by weather radar. Take shelter immediately, preferably underground

Provided by the FEMA Preparedness Guide

TAKE PROTECTITVE ACTION BEFORE A TORNADO

Be alert to changing weather conditions

- Listen to NOAA Weather Radio or to commercial radio or television newscasts for additional warnings and information
- Look for approaching storms; sometimes your own research online or by making phone calls can give you earlier heads up than normal sources on TV or radio

- Look for the following warning signs:
    - Dark, often greenish sky with thunder and lightning
    - Large hail and lots of it
    - A large, dark, low lying cloud, especially if rotating even without a funnel
    - Listen for a loud roar or growl, similar to a freight train

If you see approaching storms or any of the warning signs, be prepared to take shelter immediately, preferably underground or in the basement

DURING A TORNADO

If you are under a tornado WARNING, take shelter immediately

Disaster-Specific Preparedness Corner

If you are in:	Then:
A structure (e.g. residence, small building, school, nursing home, hospital, factory, shopping center, high-rise building)	Go to a pre-designated shelter such as a safe room, basement, storm cellar, or the lowest building level If there is no basement, go to the center of an interior room on the lowest level (closet, interior hallway) away from corners, windows, doors, and outside walls. Put as many walls as possible between you and the outside. Get under a sturdy table and use your arms to protect your head and neck. Do not open windows.
A vehicle, trailer, or mobile home	Get out immediately and go to the lowest floor of a sturdy, nearby building or a storm shelter. Mobile homes, even if tied down, offer little protection from tornadoes and even seem to attract them
The outside with no shelter	* Lie flat in a nearby ditch or depression and Cover your head with your hands. Be aware of potential flooding. * Do not get under an overpass or bridge. You are safer in a low, flat location * Never try to outrun a tornado in urban or congested areas in a vehicle. Leave it and seek safe shelter! * Watch out for flying debris. Flying debris from tornadoes causes most fatalities.

226

Disaster-Specific Preparedness Corner

Preparing a Safe Room

Extreme windstorms in many parts of the country pose a serious threat to buildings and their occupants. Your residence may be built to "code," but that does not mean it can withstand a tornado or strong winds of hurricane strength. The reason for a Safe Room is to provide a haven for yourself and your family and provide a safe refuge away from the ravages of the tornado or storm. Safe Rooms can be found in many locations in your own home.

- Your basement
- Atop a concrete slab-on-grade foundation or garage floor
- An interior room on the first floor

Safe rooms built below ground level provide the greatest protection, but a Safe Room built in a first-floor interior room also can provide adequate protection. Below-ground Safe Rooms should be designed and built to avoid accumulating water from heavy rain during a tornado hazard or hurricane.

To be able to protect you and your family, your Safe Room should be built to withstand high winds and flying debris, even if the rest of the residence is heavily damaged or even destroyed. Consider the following when building a Safe Room:

- The Safe Room must be anchored heavily to the floor or foundation to avoid being overturned or lifted up by the tornado or wind
- The walls, ceiling, and door of the shelter must withstand wind pressure and strong enough to repel falling or flying debris
- The connecting sections of the Safe Room must be strong enough to resist being torn apart
- The interior or exterior walls of the residence that make up a wall or part of the Safe Room must be structurally separated from the main structure of the rest of the house so that damage or parts of the house being blown away will not take the Safe Room with it

Disaster-Specific Preparedness Corner

There are many innovative ways to construct Safe Rooms. Go online for more information. Here's a good website reference: www.aaronsstormshelters.com.

AFTER A TORNADO

Recovering from any disaster is a gradual process. Government relief agencies will eventually get to you, but you must learn to depend on yourself and fend for yourself and not just sit around waiting to be helped. God helps those who help themselves.

Essentially, recovering from any disaster, whether it be flood, tornadoes, hurricanes, fires or earthquakes, is pretty much the same. Floods do tend to present a different sort of cleanup and recovery and cautions, as do fires; but generally recovering from any disaster requires much of the same attention. Therefore, the last section of this **Corner,** dealing with what to do after a disaster will be at the end.

HURRICANES

A hurricane is a type of tropical cyclone. In different parts of the globe they are called cyclones and typhoons. Here, in the United States they are hurricanes. We have so many that we name them each year. A typical hurricane is accompanied by severe rain storms and what the winds from the hurricane don't destroy, the rain will because it almost always causes severe flooding. In the northern hemisphere they circulate counterclockwise. In the southern hemisphere the cyclones and typhoons go the opposite direction.

All Atlantic and Gulf of Mexico coastal areas are subject to hurricanes or tropical storms. Parts of the Southwest United States and the Pacific Coast experience heavy rains and floods each year from hurricanes spawned off Mexico. The Atlantic hurricane season lasts from June to November, with the peak season from mid-August to lat October

Hurricanes can cause catastrophic damage to coastlines and several hundred miles inland if large enough ... as in Katrina. Winds may exceed 155 mph. As said in the Tornado section, sometimes Hurricanes spawn tornadoes and even microbursts, create storm surges in the ocean and cause extensive damage from heavy rainfall, not to mention flooding.

Hurricanes are classified into five categories based on their wind speed, central pressure, and damage potential. Category three and higher hurricanes are considered major hurricanes, though Categories One and Two are still extremely dangerous and warrant your full attention. Below is a chart explaining the different scales/intensities of hurricanes.

SAFFIR-SIMPSON HURRICAN SCALE *			
Scale Number (Category)	Sustained Winds (MPH)	Damage	Storm Surge
1	74 - 95	**Minimal:** Unanchored mobile homes, Vegetation, and signs	4 - 5 feet
2	96 - 110	**Moderate:** All mobile homes, roofs, & small crafts; flooding	6 - 8 feet
3	111 - 130	**Extensive:** Small buildings; low-lying roads cut off	9 – 12 feet
4	131 – 155	**Extreme:** Roofs & mobile homes destroyed, trees down, roads cut off, coastal areas flooded	13 – 18 feet
5	More than 155	**Catastrophic:** Most buildings destroy-ed, vegetation destroy-ed, major roads cut off, homes that are still stan-ding are flooded	Greater than 18 feet

* The above table taken from the FEMA Guide To Citizen Preparedness

Hurricanes can produce widespread torrential rains. Resulting floods are deadly and destructive. Slow moving storms that move into mountainous regions build up extremely heavy rain fall. Excessive rains in mountainous regions can produce mudslides, especially in areas without trees and vegetation to hold the soil in place. Flash flooding can occur and down stream, away from the storm, and people miles away from the storm will suffer the brunt of the flash floods. Heavy water flow in rivers and streams may also continue for days or weeks after the storm has subsided.

Between 1970 and 1999, more people lost their lives from freshwater inland flooding associated with land slides following heavy storms than from any other weather related hazard relating to hurricanes or tropical storms.

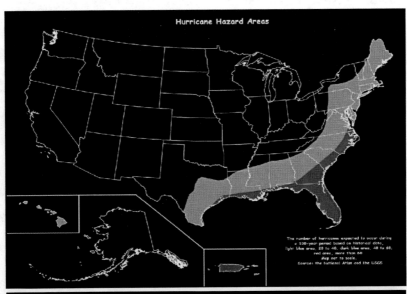

Hurricane Hazard Areas

The number of hurricanes expected to occur during a 100-year period based on historical data, light blue area, 20 to 40, dark blue area, 40 to 60, red area, more than 60.
Map not to scale.
Source: the National Atlas and the USGS

NAME THAT HURRICANE

Since 1953, hurricanes in the Atlantic have been named from lists which were put together by the National Hurricane Center. They are now maintained and updated by the World Meteorological Organization. Until 1979, when women began to complain that they were being unfairly discriminated against, all hurricanes were named after women. Now, names are male and female. Six lists are used in rotation which means the 2001 lists began again in 2007

The only time a name is changed/replace is when a hurricane is so damaging and catastrophic, it would be inappropriate for reasons of sensitivity to those who suffered great losses to use the same name again; such as the name Katrina.

However, some names are changed randomly, such as Luis being replaced by Lorenzo, or Marilyn being replaced by Michelle. A complete list of hurricane names can be found by going to the web-site www.nhe.noaa.gov under "Storm Names."

Disaster-Specific
Preparedness Corner

KNOW THE TERMS

Become familiar with the following terms to help you identify a hurricane hazard

Tropical Depression
A storm system of thick, dark clouds and thunderstorms with a ground circulation and maximum sustained wind strength of 38 mph or less. Sustained winds means a one minute average wind measured about 33 feet above the surface.

Tropical Storm
An organized storm system of strong thunderstorms with a surface circulation and a maximum sustained wind of 39-73 mph.

Hurricane
An intense tropical weather system of strong thunderstorms with a well defined surface circulation and maximum sustained wind of 74 mph or higher.

Storm Surge
A dome of water pushed ashore by hurricane and tropical storm winds. Storm surges can reach 25 feet high and be 50-100 miles wide.

Storm Tide
A combination of storm surge and the normal tide (ie., a 15-foot storm surge combined with a 2-foot normal high tide over the mean sea level creates a 17-foot storm tide.)

Hurricane/Tropical Storm Watch
Hurricane/tropical storm conditions are possible in the specified area, usually within 36 hours. Tune in to NOAA Weather Radio, commercial radio, or TV

Hurricane/Tropical Storm Warning
Hurricane/tropical storm conditions are expected in the specified area, usually within 24 hours.

Short Term Watches and Warnings
These warnings provide detailed information about specific hurricane threats, such as flash floods and tornadoes.

This information taken from the FEMA Guide To Citizen Preparedness manual

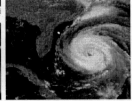

Disaster-Specific Preparedness Corner

BEFORE A HURRICANE

To prepare for a hurricane, please consider the following:

- Take measures to secure your property by boarding up windows and doors. Use at least 5/8" thick marine plywood. Cut the plywood to size if you can, but if you don't have time, slap up and nail the plywood in place anyway, it will be better than nothing. If you are able, install permanent shutters. Crossing windows with tape does NOT prevent windows from breaking.

- Install straps or additional clips to your roof to reduce roof damage. This probably should be done by someone familiar with the procedure.

- Keep trees and shrubs around your home well trimmed. This reduces wind friction (wind catching the trees/shrubs and blowing them into your home)

- Keep your rain gutters and downspouts clear of leaves and other debris.

- If you have a boat, if possible, remove your boat to another secure location.

- Consider building a safe room (discussed earlier in this **Corner**)

With today's technology, we are warned of a hurricane hazard well in advance of its landfall and we should take advantage of this time to get prepared and secure our property.

Disaster-Specific
Preparedness Corner

DURING A HURRICANE

When a hurricane is eminent, you should take the following precautions:

- Listen to the weather reports on radio and/or TV for the hurricane's progress
- Be sure your home is secure as instructed above; secure outdoor objects or bring them inside to keep them from flying around or getting damaged
- Turn off all utilities as instructed by the authorities; otherwise set your refrigerator's thermostat to its coldest and making sure it remains closed & unplug appliances and TV/radio prior to leaving your home … if you have to leave; lightning strikes on power poles will transfer electrical surges through the power and telephone lines
- Turn off your propane tanks, including the one to your grill
- Avoid using land-line phones except for serious emergencies
- If you have a boat in a marina, moor it securely or remove it to a more secure location if you have time
- Keep a supply of water for sanitary purposes and flushing toilets; fill bathtub and other large containers with water

If the following conditions are present, you should evacuate:

- If you are instructed by authorities to do so. If you are reasonably sure you will have to evacuate, even if you haven't been told to, get outa Dodge and get a jump on the crowds
- If you live in a mobile home or other temporary structure, no matter how well they are fastened to the ground

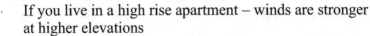

- If you live in a high rise apartment – winds are stronger at higher elevations
- If you live on the coast, or in a flood plain, river or inland body of water
- If you just feel you want to leave because you have a good sense of danger

If you are unable to evacuate, go to the safest room in your home; if you do not have a safe room, consider the following:

- Do not leave your house during the hurricane; stay away from windows and glass doors
- Secure and brace outside doors and close all interior doors
- Keep blinds and curtains closed around doors and windows as they will keep glass from flying further into the house if they break; if the wind subsides, you are probably inside the eye of the storm and it is passing overhead; when the winds return they will be coming from the opposite direction because you will be on the other side of the hurricane
- Seek out the interior room that is a closet, hallway or bathroom on the lowest level of the house; a basement is the best room to seek refuge if you have one
- Lie under a strong table or other sturdy object

See the last section for dealing with recovering after disasters

LIGHTNING

Lightning can be very dangerous; from killing you to starting fires. In the United States an average of 300 people are injured and 80 are killed each year from lightning strikes, not to mention the number of fires started. It's obvious that most people survive lightning strikes, but most suffer debilitating symptoms and injuries.

Lightning is associated not only with the everyday thunderstorm (hence the name thunder … storm), but with other major storms ie., tornadoes, hurricanes, hail storms etc. Lightning will also occur without rain or any moisture at all, even on a seemingly calm day with very few clouds. This is called dry lightning. This occurs predominately in the western part of the dry dessert areas. Rain will come from the thunder clouds, but because it is so hot, the rain evaporates before it hits the ground. Without the rain, lightning striking the ground will cause fires instantly because there is no rain to extinguish it.

SOME PRECAUTIONS TO CONSIDER FOR SAFETY WHEN LIGHTNING IS PRESENT

Lightning can strike twice in the same spot. If you are caught out in the wild, seek the lowest possible depression, but watch for flash flooding. If you are in a forest, again seek low areas under a thick growth of small trees. Standing under a large/tall tree may attract lightning and even though you are not in contact with the tree, if lightning does strike the tree, you will suffer serious injury because the lightning travels down the trunk of the tree and out through the roots and ground immediately surrounding the tree.

If you are in a boat out on a lake, go immediately to land and seek shelter inside a building if possible, or inside your car or pickup. If

you are caught on a golf course open area, again find a low spot. you feel the hair on your head end, this is an indication is about to strike. Immediately down, staying on the balls of duck your head between your hold your hands over your ears, yourself as small a target as DO NOT lie flat on the ground,

or other Anytime stand on lightning squat your feet, knees and making possible. keep as

minimal contact with the ground as possible (hence squatting on the balls of your feet).

Disaster-Specific
Preparedness Corner

Here are some facts about lightning and guidelines to follow in a lightning/thunderstorm:

- Stay indoors or get into an automobile; rubber-soled shoes/boots do not offer any protection and the wheels of the automobile (being rubber) also afford no protection, it is the steel top and body of the car that protects you if you aren't touching any metal
- Avoid showering or bathing as plumbing may conduct electricity from the house being struck
- Use cordless phones or a cell phone unless a severe emergency is present
- Unplug your TV and radio and other household appliances and air conditioners as power surges from striking a power line will damage them
- Tune to your NOAA radio, commercial TV or radio
- Natural lightning rods should be avoided such as: tall, isolated trees in an open area, hilltops, open fields, the beach or boat on water, isolated sheds or other small structure in open areas
- Anything metal – tractors, farm equipment, motorcycles, golf carts, golf clubs and bicycles and lastly … cowboys on a horse out in the open, attract lightning

Some helpful hints when giving first-aid to anyone struck by lightning:

- Anyone struck by lightning is not "charged" by the lightning and therefore is safe to administer first aid
- If breathing has stopped, begin mouth-to-mouth resuscitation
- If the heart has stopped, administer CPR (one of the skills you should learn)
- If the victim has a pulse and is still breathing, look for other possible injuries check for burns and administer
- Burn treatment (look where the lightning entered and exited the body … this is where you'll find the burns). Be aware of nervous system, broken bones or loss of hearing and eyesight. Get them to a medical facility as quickly as possible

For more information regarding lightning, go to:
www.nws.noaa.gov/om/wcm/lightning.

EARTHQUAKES

Earthquakes are one of the most frightening and destructive forces of nature. Not just from the destruction from the shaking, but the aftermath. Earthquakes originate deep within the earth's crust and are the result of tectonic plates being pushed together and one slips over the other ... at least this is what scientists say, but who really knows? It really doesn't matter to you and me, except to know that they happen suddenly, without warning and can be very destructive and frightful. Because this country is now very populated, earthquakes hit inhabited areas much more than they used to. Earthquakes happen in virtually every state ... more in some, less in others.

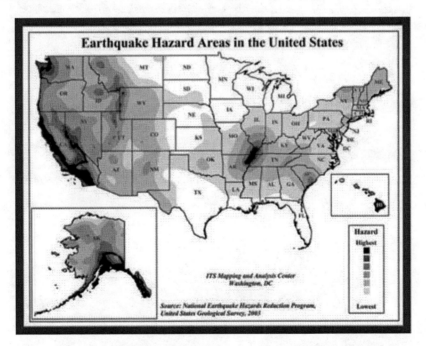

Earthquake Hazard Areas in the United States

ITS Mapping and Analysis Center
Washington, DC

Source: National Earthquake Hazards Reduction Program,
United States Geological Survey, 2003

Hazard
Highest

Lowest

Disaster-Specific Preparedness Corner

KNOW THE TERMS

Become familiar with the following terms to assist you in identifying an earthquake hazard.

Earthquake
A sudden slipping or movement of a portion of the earth's crust, accompanied and followed by a series of strong shaking or vibrations

Aftershock
An earthquake of similar or lesser intensity that follows the main jolt or shaking

Fault
The fracture across which displacement has occurred during an earthquake; the slippage may range from less than an inch to up to 10 yards in a severe earthquake

Epicenter
The place on the earth's surface directly above the point on the fault where the earthquake rupture began. Once a fault begins to slip, it expands outward along the fault line during the quaking and can extend hundreds of miles in all directions before stopping.

Seismic Waves
Vibrations that travel outwardly from the earthquake fault at speeds of several miles per second. Fault slippage directly under a structure can cause considerable damage, but the vibrations of these waves cause most of the destruction during an earthquake.

Magnitude
The amount of energy released during an earthquake, which is computed from the amplitude of the seismic waves. A magnitude of 7.0 on the Richter Scale indicates an extremely strong earthquake. Each whole number on the scale represents an increase of about 30 times more energy released than the previous whole number represents. Therefore, an earthquake measuring 6.0 is about 30 times more powerful than one that measures 5.0. The great Alaska earthquake in 1964 measured 9.2 and I was there to experience it.

BEFORE AN EARTHQUAKE
The following are things you can do to protect yourself, your family, and your property in advance of an earthquake.

- Repair defective electrical wiring, leaky gas lines, and inflexible utility connections. Get appropriate professional help, unless you are qualified
- Bolt down or secure your water heater, refrigerator, furnace and gas appliances to the floor or wall studs; if offered in your area, have your gas company install an automatic shut off valve if triggered by strong vibrations from an earthquake
- Store your glass contained food and water, especially if you do self canning from your garden etc., on the lower shelves, next to the floor; store china and other such valuables on low shelves or in cabinets that fasten securely to keep from opening during an earthquake (hey, mom's got to show off her stuff eh?)
- Securely anchor overhead lighting fixtures and ceiling fans
- Be sure your residence is securely fastened to the foundation
- Install, or have installed, flexible pipe fittings to avoid water or gas leaks.
- Locate safe spots in your house ie., under large, sturdy tables, desks or benches
- Hold earthquake drills with your family; drop, cover and hold on (and don't forget to pray)

DURING AN EARTHQUAKE
Minimize your movements during an earthquake to a few steps to a nearby safe place. Stay indoors until the shaking has subsided and you are sure it is safe to venture outside. During the earthquake in Alaska, I was walking home from JC Penny's. I was totally

Disaster-Specific
Preparedness Corner

unable to stand, much less walk, so I held on to a nearby tree. The quaking lasted for over five minutes!

The streets were so mangled; people got out of their cars and walked with me. Panic was everywhere; mayhem was the order of the day. Because of the confusion and the streets being torn up, it took me several hours to make my way back home, when it should have only taken me about another hour. Most don't experience a quake of this magnitude

Disaster-Specific Preparedness Corner

IF YOU ARE:	THEN:
Indoors	• Take cover under a sturdy table, desk, bench or against an in-side wall, and hold on. If there isn't a table, or desk near you, cover your face and head with your arms and crouch in an inside corner of the building • Stay away from glass, windows, outside doors and walls, and anything that could fall, such as furniture or lighting fixtures • Stay in bed – if you are there when the earthquake strikes – hold on and protect your head with a pillow, unless you are under a heavy light fixture or fan that could fall, if so, move to a safer place • Use a doorway for shelter only if it is in close proximity to you and if you know it is a strongly supported, load-bearing doorway • Stay inside until the shaking stops and it is safe to go outside; most injuries occur when people run into or out of buildings and are hit by falling objects • Be aware that the electricity may go out or the sprinkler systems or fire alarms may turn on • Do NOT use the elevators Remember, even after buildings have ceased swaying, they may still be dangerous from collapsing, so keep away from them
Outdoors	• Stay there • Move away from buildings, streetlights, and utility poles
In a moving vehicle	• Stop as quickly as safety permits and stay in the vehicle; a-void stopping near or under buildings, trees, overpasses, and utility wires • Proceed cautiously once the earthquake has stopped; watching for road and bridge damage
Trapped under debris	• Do not light a match, no matter how bad you want to smoke • Do not move about, kicking up dust • If you can, cover your mouth with a handkerchief or cloth • Tap on a pipe or wall so rescuers can locate you, calling out if you feel someone is near enough to hear you; whistle if you can • Be careful of breathing in dust from what the debris has kicked up, so don't get excited, try to remain calm so you are not breathing heavily

Disaster-Specific Preparedness Corner

AFTER AN EARTHQUAKE – CAUTIONS TO TAKE THAT ARE UNIQUE TO EARTHQUAKES

- Always expect aftershocks; secondary shakes are usually less violent and each successive quake will be less than the last; aftershocks can still do additional damage and continue to weaken structures
- When opening cabinets and closets, be careful as objects will fall off shelves
- Stay away from damaged buildings, unless your help is requested by police, fire or rescue personnel or relief organizations
- If you live close to coastal areas, be aware of tidal waves/tsunamis, also known as seismic waves; when a tsunami warnings are given, always assume that a series of dangerous waves is on the way; stay away from the beach and seek higher ground (remember Indonesia in December of 2004)

After the great Alaska earthquake in 1964, the tsunami that hit Valdez did so much damage that they moved the entire town to another location. Most of the fatalities in this earthquake were caused by the tsunami in Valdez.

caused by the tsunami in Valdez.

EXTREME COLD AND HEAT

BEFORE WINTER STORMS AND EXTREME COLD

For those of you who live in areas where you can have large amounts of snow and very cold temperatures (which is not restricted to Alaska), you should have in your disaster supplies kit:

- Rock salt or ice melt to clear walkways; rock salt is also good to carry in your car emergency kit because by throwing rock salt under your tires if stuck, will melt the ice AND give your tires traction
- Bags of sand to enhance the rock salt in improving traction in your vehicle
- Snow shovels and other snow removal equipment ie., snow blower, snowplow

Disaster-Specific Preparedness Corner

In times of severe winter storms, you might find yourself isolated and/or cut off in your home, so always stock up on hand extra heating fuel or wood for a fireplace or wood burning stove and keep your propane tank on the upper side of half full. If you are connected to natural gas, chances are you will still have service, but in case you don't, have an alternative heat source such as a wood burning stove but never, ever heat with it inside your home without a smokestack to the outside; carbon monoxide will kill you, so never burn any open flame in your house without a smokestack venting the smoke to the outside.

Winterize your home by adding extra insulation in the attic and walls. Caulk up cracks in doors and windows and add weather stripping around them as well. Install storm windows or replace existing windows with thermal pane windows.

Winterize your car by doing the following:

- Check your batter and ignition system; be sure the battery is fully charged and in top condition; keep battery cables and posts free of corrosion
- Keep anti-freeze levels at maximum; make sure your anti-freeze is sufficient enough to guard against freezing at the coldest temperatures in your area
- Make sure your heater and defroster works efficiently and properly
- Be sure your wipers are in good condition and keep your washer fluid full and of the type that will not freeze; keep all systems in your car working properly.
- Check your thermostat; make sure it works properly because if it doesn't, your heater/defroster won't work properly
- Consider installing a circulating heater or head-bolt heater in your car; this device allows you to "plug-in" your vehicle to keep the engine and oil warm to allow the engine to turn over properly for easy starting.

Disaster-Specific Preparedness Corner

When I was a kid living in Alaska, I remember the troubles my father had in keeping our vehicles in good condition and keeping them running in the winter. It seemed that cold weather always brought out the worst in a vehicle. It would be so cold sometimes that we could get the old Ford started, but it wouldn't move because the grease in the wheels was so thick from the cold. Then, after getting it started and moving, it moved very slowly and the tires on the bottom sides were flat and didn't round out until we had traveled some distance. The speed didn't pick up and the thumping didn't cease for a few miles. Modern tires and vehicles today don't suffer from extremely cold weather as ours did back in the 50's and 60's. In any case, your vehicles should be kept in good order for when cold weather hits.

DURING A WINTER STORM AND EXTREME COLD

Some great advice and cautions for what you should do in the event you are caught in a severe winter storm or extreme temperatures:

- Always listen to your NOAA radio, commercial radio or TV for updates and information (heck, when I was a kid we would just look out the window and checked the thermometer)
- Eat regularly and drink plenty of fluids but avoid alcohol and caffeine; cold weather will dry you out and alcohol and caffeine speeds up the process
- While shoveling snow, avoid over exhaustion, especially if you have heart trouble; using a snow blower is always best, but if you must shovel by hand, be very careful and don't over exert
- Watch for signs of frostbite; loss of feeling (after hurting a whole bunch for some time) and white or pale skin; pay particular attention to parts of the skin exposed to the cold ie., ears, nose; fingers, even inside gloves or mittens will be affected as well as toes; mittens will keep hands warmer than gloves because the

Disaster-Specific
Preparedness Corner

· fingers are next to each other and will help keep each other warm; get medical help immediately if you suspect frost bite; you will definitely have frost bite if the affected area's skin turns black … then amputation will almost always result

Hypothermia is due to the loss of body heat; signs consist of shivering uncontrollably, memory loss, disorientation, incoherence, slurring of speech, drowsiness, and of course exhaustion; get the victim so afflicted to a warm place, remove wet clothing, warm the center of the body first and administer warm, non-alcoholic beverages if the victim is conscious; if unconscious, remove clothing down to the skin and remove your clothing down to the skin as well and climb in between the covers with the victim, holding them tightly against you, your front to their back (an old Boy Scout remedy); heating pads and electric blankets are effective as well; get medical attention to the victim as soon as possible

· Conserve fuel by lowering the temperature of your home and don a sweater, wool socks and wear a hat; temporarily close off heat in some rooms if you can
· Maintain ventilation if using kerosene heaters to avoid build-up of toxic fumes; refuel heaters outside the home and keep them at least three feet from any flames or flammable objects
· If you must drive, travel during daylight hours, don't travel alone; keep others informed of your travel plans and stay in contact with them; be sure to take your vehicle emergency kit with you; stay on main roads and avoid shortcuts

Sometimes you hear of people being stranded on highways and roads by blinding blizzards. If you get caught, pull over and turn on your hazard lights. Do not leave your vehicle unless you see a building and know you can reach it safely and take shelter. Unless you have warm footwear and clothing, don't attempt to walk to a building even if you can see it.

Keep your vehicle's fuel on the upper side of half during winter months. If you are caught in a blizzard, run your car's engine for 10 minutes every hour to keep warm. Be sure to clear snow away from the exhaust pipe and keep your car window cracked for ventilation in case carbon monoxide comes into the cabin.

Do light exercising to generate body heat. Take turns sleeping with your partner and drink fluids to keep from dehydrating yourself. After dark, turn the interior light on so rescue crews can see you and balance battery power with electrical needs. Now is a good time to use your cell phone.

If stranded out in the open, after the blizzard has passed, stomp out SOS in the snow with the letters being 15' high and at least four feet wide separated by two feet. Leave the car and proceed on foot if necessary but only if you have proper winter clothing and footwear.

Follow the instructions for recovering from this disaster in the last section in this **Corner.**

Disaster-Specific
Preparedness Corner

UNDERSTANDING EXTREME HEAT

Heat kills by pushing the human body beyond its limits. Extreme heat, even during high humidity you will find that evaporation is slowed, but the body must work harder to maintain its normal temperature.

Most heat victims are harmed because they have been overexposed to the heat or have over-exerted themselves for their age, physical condition and health and for not rehydrating often. Elderly, young children, sick persons and overweight people are more likely to suffer and succumb from extreme and extended exposure to heat.

Heat related illnesses can be onset by stagnant or un-circulating or contaminated air. Consequently, people who live in highly populated urban areas will be affected more and for longer periods. Asphalt and concrete add to the problem because they absorb and retain heat and release it during the night which causes nighttime temperatures to remain higher without cooling.

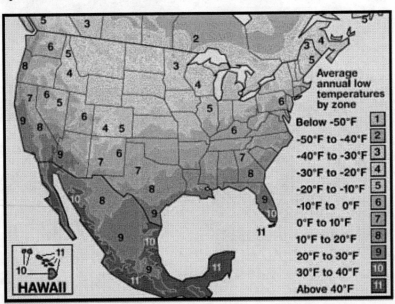

Average annual low temperatures by zone

Below -50°F	1
-50°F to -40°F	2
-40°F to -30°F	3
-30°F to -20°F	4
-20°F to -10°F	5
-10°F to 0°F	6
0°F to 10°F	7
10°F to 20°F	8
20°F to 30°F	9
30°F to 40°F	10
Above 40°F	11

HAWAII

Disaster-Specific Preparedness Corner

KNOW THE TERMS

Familiarize yourself with these terms to help identify an extreme heat hazard

HEAT WAVE
Prolonged period of excessive heat, often combined with excessive humidity.

HEAT INDEX
A number in degrees Fahrenheit (F) that tells how hot it feels when relative humidity is added to the air temperature. Exposure to full sunshine can increase the het index by 15 degrees.

HEAT CRAMPS
Muscular pains and spasms due to heavy exertion. Although heat cramps are the least severe, they are often the first signal that the body is having trouble with the heat.

HEAT EXHAUSTION
Typically occurs when people exercise heavily or work in a hot, humid place where body fluids are lost through perspiration. Blood flow to the skin increases, causing blood flow to decrease to the vital organs. This results in a form of mild shock. If not treated, the victim's condition will worsen. Body temperature will keep rising and the victim may suffer heat stroke.

HEAT STROKE
A life-threatening condition. The victim's temperature control system, which produces sweating to cool the body, stops working. The body temperature can rise so high that brain damage and death may result if the body is not cooled quickly.

SUN STROKE
Another term for heat stroke. Both very severe and life threatening.

BEFORE EXTREME HEAT

Take protective measures

- Install window air conditioners snugly; insulate if necessary

Disaster-Specific
Preparedness Corner

- Check air-conditioning ducts for proper insulation and for obstructions
- Install temporary window reflectors such as aluminum foil-covered cardboard to reflect heat back outside; install sun/heat reflective film over windows
- Weather-strip doors and sills to keep cool air in
- Install blinds, louvers or outdoor awnings over windows that receive morning or afternoon sun (outdoor awnings can reduce heat that enters the home by 80%)

DURING EXTREME HEAT

Follow these guidelines for avoiding extreme heat problems

- Stay indoors as much as possible and limit exposure to the sun
- If air-conditioning is unavailable, stay on the lowest floor possible, or in the basement
- Consider spending the hottest time of the day in public, air-conditioned buildings such as shopping malls, movie theaters and other community facilities
- Eat well-balanced meals that are light with little meat (meat speeds up your metabolism and creates heat), eating cool fruits and drinking lots of fluids, not coffee or alcohol; avoid using salt tablets unless directed otherwise by your physician
- People with epilepsy, heart, kidney or liver disease or on fluid restricted diets, or have problems with fluid retention should consult their physician before increasing fluid intake
- Dress in loose-fitting, light weight and light colored clothes that cover as much skin as possible
- Wear a wide-brimmed hat when out of doors
- Never leave children or pets in closed vehicles

Disaster-Specific Preparedness Corner

- Avoid strenuous work during the warmest part of the day; take frequent drinking breaks and use the buddy system when working in extreme heat conditions
- Check on family, friends and neighbors who do not have air-conditioning and who spend much of their time alone

Some First-Aid for Heat-Induced Illness

Condition	Symptoms	First-Aid
Sunburn	Skin redness and pain, possible swelling, blisters, fever, headaches	• Take a shower using soap to remove oils that may block pores, preventing the body from cooling naturally • Apply dry, sterile dressings to any blisters, and get medical attention
Heat Cramps	Painful spasms, usually in leg and abdominal muscles; heavy sweating	• Get the victim to a cooler location • Lightly stretch and gently massage affected muscles to relieve spasms • Give sips of up to a half glass of cool water every 15 minutes (Do not give liquids with caffeine or alcohol) • Discontinue liquids, if victim is nauseated
Heat Exhaustion	Heavy sweating but skin may be cool, pale, or flushed; weak pulse; normal body temperature is possible, but temperature will likely rise; fainting or dizziness, nausea, vomiting, exhaustion, and headaches are possible.	• Get victim to lie down in a cool place • Loosen or remove clothing • Apply cool, wet cloths • Fan or move victim to air-conditioned place • Give sips of water if victim is conscious • Be sure water is consumed slowly • Give half glass of cool water every 15 minutes • Discontinue water if victim is nauseated • Seek immediate medical attention if vomiting occurs
Heat Stroke (a severe medical emergency)	High body temperature (105° +); hot, red, dry skin; rapid, weak pulse; shallow breathing; victim will probably not sweat unless was sweating from recent strenuous activity possible unconsciousness	• Call 9-1-1 or emergency medical services, or get the victim to a hospital immediately; **Do not delay** • Move victim to a cooler environment • Remove clothing • Try a cool bath, sponging, or wet sheet to reduce body temperature • Watch for breathing problems • Use extreme caution • Use fans and air-conditioners

Prolonged drought and poor water supply management, or not taking precautions outlined above to avoid over exertion in the heat, can be instrumental in causing emergencies. Drought and extreme heat can affect large regions of the country and in turn, fires and flash flooding can be an effect of drought and extreme heat conditions. Protecting your life and the life of your loved ones is paramount in this, and any other emergency.

We have attempted to include in this **Corner,** the most frequent disasters that we inhabitants of the United States, Canada and Mexico will most likely be exposed to; or in other words, that are the most frequent. Other disasters include wild fires, volcano eruptions and mud and dirt slides. Much of what has been discussed here covers the preparations necessary for us to deal with these other disasters. Being prepared is the most comforting of all.

This last section will take into account what steps and actions should be taken after most disasters. There is a commonality with all disasters in their aftermath.

RECOVERING FROM DISASTER

Health and Safety Guidelines

Recovering from a disaster is usually a gradual process. Safety is a primary issue, as are mental and physical well-being. If assistance is available, knowing how to access it makes the process faster and less stressful. This section offers some general advice on steps to take after disaster strikes in order to begin getting your home, your community and your family back to normal as soon as possible.

AIDING THE INURED

Check for injuries. Do not attempt to move seriously injured persons unless they are in immediate danger of death or further injury. If you must move an injured person and they are

are unconscious, stabilize the neck and back, then call for help immediately. Just this alone gives rise to a very big reason you should be involved in CERT or Red Cross training. After all, the life you save may be one of your family.

- If the victim is not breathing, carefully position and prepare (clear airway) them in a manner for you to administer CPR
- Maintain body temperatures with blankets; taking care to not overheat victim
- Never try to administer liquids to an unconscious victim

HEALTH
- Be aware of exhaustion; do not attempt too much at one time; set priorities and pace yourself; get enough rest
- Drink plenty of clean water
- Eat well
- Wash or sanitize your hands thoroughly and often when working in debris
- Wear sturdy work boots, gloves, protective goggles and hat (hard, if available)

SAFETY ISSUES
- Be aware of new safety issues created by the disaster; watch for washed out roads, contaminated buildings, contaminated water, gas leaks, broken glass, potential for falling debris
- Inform local authorities about health and safety issues, including chemical spills, downed power lines, washed out roads, smoldering insulation or other debris, dead animal

RETURNING HOME

Returning to your home can be both physically and mentally challenging and exhausting, exacerbated by the surrounding carnage. Above all, use extreme caution, especially upon entering

Disaster-Specific
Preparedness Corner

your home after a disaster. Be cautious not only of fallen debris, contamination, gas leaks, exposed electrical wiring etc., but looters as well. Many ne'er-do-wells prey upon people during disasters because during emergencies, people are usually exhausted, ill-prepared and frightened. Exercise your right to keep and bear arms to protect yourself and family. The mere presence of an armed citizen is usually enough to frighten off potential looters.

- Keep a battery-powered or hand crank radio with you so you can listen for emergency updates and further warnings; keep a battery-powered flashlight handy (Caution: Light your flashlight outside before entering any building as it might cause a spark, igniting leaking gas)
- Watch out for animals that might have holed up in your home during the disaster, especially in areas where there are poisonous snakes; use a pole to poke into debris
- If your phone is working, cell or land line, use only for life threatening situations
- Stay off the streets; if you must go out, watch for falling objects such as power poles, trees, signs etc., electrical wires, weakened walls, bridges

BEFORE ENTERING YOUR HOME
Walk carefully around the outside and check for loose power lines, gas leaks, and structural damage. If you have any doubts about safely entering, DON'T. Have your residence inspected by a qualified building inspector or engineer before entering

Do not enter if: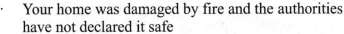
- You smell gas
- Floodwaters remain around the structure
- Your home was damaged by fire and the authorities have not declared it safe

Before you go inside your home, there are certain things you should and should not do. Do enter your home carefully during daylight hours and check for damage. Be aware of loose boards and slippery floors. The following list is what you should do upon entering:

- If you smell gas or hear a hissing noise, vacate the home and shut off the outside gas feed; call the gas company; do not lite matches or do anything that may cause a spark
- Check for frayed or loose electrical wiring; do not attempt to touch or move the wiring; notify the electrical company
- Check roof , foundation and chimney for cracks, loose bricks etc.; if it looks like any of these might fail, leave immediately
- If appliances are wet or in standing water, do not touch; turn off main power switch; have power company check electrical wiring to ensure it is safe to have the power on
- If water or sewer lines are damaged and/or leaking, turn off main water valve; have authorities check for contaminated wells and integrity of your septic system or sewer line
- Throw out all food and other supplies that you suspect may have become contaminated, either by the disaster or animals/insects

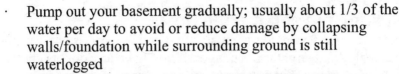

Disaster-Specific
Preparedness Corner

- Pump out your basement gradually; usually about 1/3 of the water per day to avoid or reduce damage by collapsing walls/foundation while surrounding ground is still waterlogged
- When opening cabinets, be careful of falling contents
- Clean up household chemical spills ie., Drano, soaps, turpentine, paint, oil
- Call your insurance agent; take pictures of damage; keep good records of cleanup and repairs

Disasters also have a devastating effect on animals. Some following hints will help in dealing with not only wild animals, but domesticated animals as well as they will also be under a lot of stress:

- Do not approach or attempt to help an injured or stranded animal; call your local animal control services or wildlife resource officer
- Do not corner animals or try to rescue them; wild animals especially will likely feel threatened and are in a defensive mode already and may harm themselves and you by trying to escape
- If you find animals in your home upon returning, open doors and windows and give them an avenue of escape; animals will most generally leave on their own accord when humans approach; if not, contact your local animal control or wildlife officer
- Do not attempt to move a dead animal, it may be infected and cause a serious health risk; contact your health department or local animal control or wildlife officer
- If bitten by any animal, seek immediate medical attention

In severe disasters the federal government will join with the state and local governments to offer assistance. However, as in Katrina, the devastation was so widespread and so many people affected, help was slow in coming and short on assistance.

Therefore, it behooves all of us to be prepared, well prepared, to cope with disaster. Preparation does not always end with food, water, first aid, clothing, supplies etc., but also psychological. No matter how strong or experienced you may be in coping with disaster, everyone suffers from post traumatic stress. Stress will be greatly reduced if you are prepared with food, water etc.

After a disaster, it is normal to feel anxious and sad and full of grief. These are human emotions and do serve their purpose. Acknowledge your feelings, focus on your strengths and abilities and get involved in helping other family members, neighbors and your community. This will help keep your mind of your own problems. Accept help when offered.

You can contact your local counselor and even for professional with someone about your sorrow etc. Do not blame steps to promote your emotional healing by exercise, relaxation and if medication prescribed by get back to and maintain daily routines and limit responsibilities on family. Spend time with Participate in memorials.

religious advisor or volunteer agencies counseling. Talk feelings —anger, yourself and take own physician and healthy eating, rest, necessary, your doctor. Try to normal family and demanding yourself and your family and friends.

Disasters can leave children feeling frightened, confused, and insecure. Whether a child has personally experienced trauma, has merely seen the event on television, or has heard it being discussed by adults, it is important for parents and teachers to be informed and ready to help if reactions to stress begin to occur. A good religious/spiritual upbringing and example is also helpful for children and adults.

Express your faith to one another and to your children. Exercise faith and know that God is aware of all His children ... you and me.

Disaster-Specific Preparedness Corner

Much of this **Corner** was quoted or taken directly out of the *FEMA Guide To Citizen Preparedness* manual. We have taken care to simplify even this information so as not to overwhelm the reader and to show that a systematic plan for preparation is possible and should be accomplished BEFORE the disaster strikes. Get 'er done!

This chapter was researched, edited and compiled by my husband Lonnie Crockett

Outdoor Survival Corner

Outdoor Survival Corner

Simple steps to help you with this corner.

1. Acquire outdoor shelter i.e., tent, tarp, rope, waterproofing; sturdy, warm clothing, adequate footwear, hats, gloves and jackets

2. Acquire fire starting implements i.e., waterproof matches, flint or magnesium and steel, learn to make a bow drill, keep fire starting material (lint, shavings) in dry container

3. Learn where water sources are located in your are before a disaster strikes

4. Learn about and acquire information on edible plants and wild game for your area

5. Acquire campfire cooking pots/pans, learn to use them; practice recipes; learn to cook over open fire with no pots/pans

6. Acquire and keep First-Aid kit in your emergency pack, learn CPR and basic first aid skills; understand basic safety skills to avoid injury

7. Become familiar with sanitation practices; learn poisonous plants & insects; acquire knowledge for outdoor hygiene

8. Learn and practice knot tying and for which purpose each knot is designed

9. Acquire a Boy Scout manual to assist in outdoor skills; practice makes perfect

10. Keep it simple, don't get overwhelmed and have FUN!

Outdoor Survival Discussion

In an age of modern society characterized by leisure, push button this, push button that and the ability to just drive down to the store in our air-conditioned automobile and purchase whatever we want, we have gotten away from even the basic skills necessary to survive outdoors if we were forced to live outdoors. Modern-day conveniences and not having to worry about survival, our attention has been turned to leisure, easy living, convenience, abundance and we have forgotten how to even start a fire without a match. Consequently, people have not developed the skills which could enable them to survive stresses encountered in the wilds. History is full of stories of how people were one day living in luxury and the next being forced out of their homes and fend for themselves in the great out of doors

Necessity is the mother of invention. However, I hope this **Corner** will instill some thinking of the *necessity* to learn some basic outdoor survival skills. Old Eagle Boy Scouts, such as myself, still remember many of the things we learned while being a Boy Scout, and in my case, I still use skills learned while scouting ie., tying knots, outdoor camping and cooking etc. Besides, it can be fun and enjoyable to learn some of the basic skills even if we never have to use them … and hopefully we won't [have to].

Short of war or nuclear attack (which constitutes war in my opinion) or nuclear accident over a huge area, we will only have to survive outdoors for a limited period of time. Natural disasters always come to an end. It's the aftermath that causes the problem ie., clean up, re-building, locating family members (see Communication and Family Location Corner) because while we may not be able to relocate to our communities, neighborhoods or even our homes, it will be necessary to have at least some basic outdoor skills to tide us over until emergency relief systems can be put into place. Some disasters will cause widespread damage and overwhelm relief agencies. So, be prepared … isn't this what this book is all about? Let's get 'er done!

Outdoor Survival Corner

Outdoor Survival Discussion

Word has it that the average American's duration quotient, while camping in a tent and having to build a cooking fire and going to the bathroom in the out of doors, is but three days. We begin longing for the conveniences of turning on a light, drawing hot water from a faucet, flushing toilet, TV, no mosquitoes and on and on and on. Some die hard hunters will go out for longer periods of time, but usually with a camp trailer or other modern convenience. However, being thrust out into the wilderness without these luxury items could be disastrous without some basic skills to aid us in our survival. My X-wife wouldn't go camping unless I took a generator and an electric blanket with us. Then, she coerced me into getting a motor home. Well, camping was over as far as I was concerned. Can't build a campfire in the motor home, but you can take a warm shower………..ahhhhhhh!

While still living in Alaska (lived there the first 30 years of my life) my father hated hunting and fishing in the summer and fall because if he was bitten by a mosquito it would swell up and be very painful, so I did all the fishing and we hunted during the winter hunt (in those days there were two moose hunts … fall and winter). He used to jokingly say that roughing it for him was staying in a Motel 6.

Outdoor Survival Corner

Outdoor Survival Discussion

Many camp sites today are equipped with brick fire pits, outhouses, electrical and sewer hookups for camp trailers and motor homes, groomed tent sites, picnic benches and even running water. This is the modern way to camp. Not many skills are needed to camp in this fashion

Outdoor Survival Corner

SHELTER

One of the very first skills one should learn is how to construct a shelter to protect yourself from the elements. It won't matter how much food, water, or other supplies you have on hand, if you are exposed to the elements … heat, cold, wind, rain or snow, you won't be able to survive. A basic rope tied between two trees with a tarp, plastic sheeting and even a space blanket, and rocks around the edges to hold it down, is a quick set up and will suffice until a more sturdy and lasting shelter can be constructed.

Another somewhat easy shelter is the Dugout shelter. This can be dug out of the side of a hill … barring any hills, you can even dig a hole on the flat. Digging it out on the side of a hill, preferably near the top to avoid run off from rain entering your shelter, is the best of all locations. First, look for a depression in the ground. The size of the depression will likely be the size of your shelter, so shop around. (Note: You can always dig it out bigger, but the goal is to expend as little energy as possible; preserving it for other necessary activities)

SHELTER

Clear out all the leaves and debris, setting it aside to use for the interior (if the debris is dry, that is). Find large branches and fallen deadwood and drag them over the hole. Cover with leaves, brush and possibly soil, scooped out from the shelter hole. If you have a tarp, cover the deadwood and branches with that, taking care not to poke holes in the tarp and then place the leaves, brush and soil over the top. Build a nice fire about 5 feet in front of the shelter and presto, you have a warm and comfortable shelter.

A healthy human can survive many days without food and several days without water, but in many cases can only survive a few hours without shelter. Plan your shelter to coincide with the type of weather you might encounter while "holing up" in the wilds.

If there are a lot of dead saplings or large branches around, you could form a teepee and cover it with more brush and smaller branches and even a tarp if you have one. With the hole in the center at the top, it is even convenient to build a fire inside and to cook on and warm the interior. Snow would be blocked from coming in through the small cracks and openings, but rain would find itself inside unless the teepee was covered with a tarp.

SHELTER

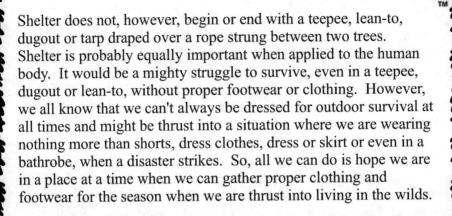

Shelter does not, however, begin or end with a teepee, lean-to, dugout or tarp draped over a rope strung between two trees. Shelter is probably equally important when applied to the human body. It would be a mighty struggle to survive, even in a teepee, dugout or lean-to, without proper footwear or clothing. However, we all know that we can't always be dressed for outdoor survival at all times and might be thrust into a situation where we are wearing nothing more than shorts, dress clothes, dress or skirt or even in a bathrobe, when a disaster strikes. So, all we can do is hope we are in a place at a time when we can gather proper clothing and footwear for the season when we are thrust into living in the wilds.

When in survival mode, forget about surviving while remaining "green." While it may be great advice for a camp site provided by your town or state to stress low impact on the environment, the environment should be your last concern in a survival situation. You will be living at odds with the environment and nature. It will be the environment that kills you. Use your intellect as your primary weapon AGAINST nature. In a survival situation your concern is that YOU and YOURS survive … you are the animal … everything else is potential food or materials.

Keep on hand water repellent foot gear with high tops and soles with good walking/hiking tread. Socks should be the kind that will wick away moisture. Have long pants and shirts that will stand up to the rigors of living outdoors such as rip-stop fabric. Have a hat that can be battened down so that it remains on your head. One that has a wide brim for shading the face and neck and will shed water. Have a light jacket that will shed water and light weight rain gear. Carry a heavier weight jacket and leather, and/or insulated gloves, depending on the season. In winter, living outdoors can be much more difficult, so have warmer snow boots and insulated pants and shirt with a winter jacket and hat.

SHELTER

Wool will keep you warm, even when wet, so wool clothing in winter is a good choice. A large percentage of body heat escapes through the head, so wear a warm hat.

It is not my intention here to instruct you how to dress, but rather, to make suggestions on what you should have or take with you when being out doors for a longer period of time, surviving in a tent or under a lean-to. Lastly, the clothing you wear should be durable, able to keep you warm and protected and dry. That is the main point here.

Outdoor survival gear should include at least the following after your clothing and shelter supplies:

- · Flashlight w/extra batteries
- · Small fold up type shovel

Continued -

Outdoor Survival Corner

SHELTER

- Large knife
- Hatchet or small axe for cutting branches and small trees for shelter and fire wood
- Water proof matches/fire starting magnesium and steel and/or a flint and steel; even a small magnifying glass or bow drill for starting a fire
- Fire starting material such as lint from a clothes dryer kept in a small water tight baggie; wood shavings and other easily ignited materials, also kept in a baggie
- Mess kit for cooking and eating your food
- Canteen or other water container and water purification tablets
- First-Aid kit
- Small signaling mirror and compass; map of the area you are camped in
- Length of rope (25') and strong twine (for snares)
- Some fishing line, hooks & weights (worms can be dug up for bate along stream banks and under rocks)
- Whistle for getting someone's attention
- Anything else that you can think of for your particular situation and location

A bow drill, (shown below) can be made out of a piece of cottonwood bark, a straight stick and some strong, durable twine or narrow strip of leather.

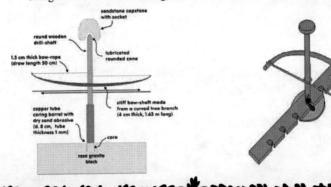

SHELTER

Magnesium fire starters will start a fire even when it is wet and cold. When a small piece of magnesium is scraped by a piece of steel, small shavings fall onto the surface of your kindling and a spark, created by shaving vigorously on the piece of magnesium, ignites the small magnesium shavings and burn very intensely and will ignite virtually any burnable material. This method of starting fires is much easier and more reliable than even flint and steel and even matches if windy.

SEARCHING FOR WATER

Another worry, especially in much of the dessert west, is the location of a good reliable water source. Many a tragedy has occurred from people getting lost in the dessert and dying of thirst. You can carry only so much water as it is very heavy, so when in the wilderness, especially in more arid areas, while you have water, search out a source to replenish your water supply. Minimum requirements for an adult are one gallon/week. (See the **Water Storage Corner** for more information on water)

Most water can be found on the sloping side of hills and mountains. The other side is usually steep and has a faster runoff from winter snows and fewer areas for trapping water. Narrow canyons should be followed up to their heads because small springs and seeps are often located at the top and will dry up after flowing only a short distance.

Digging for water is also a very good option. Look for areas where vegetation is thriving and lush while all around it is dry and very little or no vegetation, such as the base of cliffs and rocks. Dry mud holes, sinks and even dry river beads, especially at the outer bend of the river is an excellent area to dig for water. Look for large sand dunes and dig on the shady or steep side as well as anyplace where the ground is moist. You might want to search for water in old mining areas and in old mine shafts. Be sure the shaft if safe before entering. Digging a hole in a place where the soil is moist or wet is almost a sure bet as water will drain into the hole from the surrounding soil.

SEARCHING FOR WATER

Another method of collecting water is, if you have a large plastic bag, take vegetation (leaves etc) and cut it or tear it up and place it in the bag with a depression on the downward side of a hump or mound. Place it in the sun. The sun will evaporate the water from the vegetation and the water will drain to the lower depression and you will be amazed at how much water you can get from a bunch of vegetation.

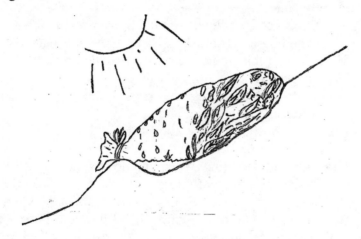

This is a simple, but effective method of extracting water from your natural surroundings when you are in desperate need of water.

Another trick is to rise just as the sun begins to peek over the mountains or horizon and take a wash cloth or other absorbent cloth, such as your neckerchief/bandana and go to where there is a lot of grass and drag it over and through the grass, collecting dew. Then, when the cloth is saturated, wring it out over your water container. You'll be surprised how much water you can collect this way. Repeat this several times before the sun dries it all up.

PRECAUTIONS USING WATER

Anyone who is inexperienced in the out of doors will want to be thrifty in the use of water. Some precautions are set out below:

- Do not eat when there is no water available – eating uses up the body's water reserve
- Store water in your stomach, not in your canteen or water bottle. People have died from dehydration with water still in their canteen
- Water polluted by animals or mud may taste awful but when you boil it vigorously for 5 minutes, it is harmless
- Muddy water that you collect will partially be cleared if you let it sit overnight, run through several thicknesses of cloth or grass filter; for this reason it is advisable to carry a small water filtering device with you
- During the heat of the day, stay still and don't do much physically and remain in the shade so as not to lose body fluids through sweating; when you do have to walk, walk slowly so you won't work up a sweat
- Placing a couple small pebbles in the mouth and taking small sips of water or chewing gum will relieve thirst, but will not stop dehydration
- The drinking of blood or urine only increases dehydration, so don't do it; soaking a cloth or your bandana in urine and wrapping around the head or neck will help cool the body and reduces evaporation

Outdoor Survival Corner

FOOD SOURCES

Once you have exhausted your emergency food supply and find that you still may have to remain in the out of doors a while longer, you should at least have some basic knowledge of edible plants in your area. Different parts of the country have a wide and extended range of edible plants. A good item to have in your outdoor survival gear should be a manual on edible plants for your area of the country. This may be found in sporting good stores or book stores. Check out the Boy Scouts of America web-site.

Some basic and common items that may be eaten and provide nutrition are listed below:

- Wild strawberries, blueberries, currants, cranberries, raspberries and blackberries and other berries common to your area of the country
- Cattail roots may be peeled and dried and ground and mixed with water and cooked to make a sort of bread; young shoots may be boiled and eaten like asparagus; the cattail heads may also be stuffed in between blankets to insulate against the cold (take the heads apart first) and stuffed into shoes or boots to prevent frostbite
- Stinging nettle may be boiled down and drunk as a tea; the milk from this plant will also relieve sunburn and contact with poison ivy or oak
- Wild onions or garlic may be eaten and also crushed and rubbed over the skin to prevent insect bites
- Rose hips may be eaten raw or boiled to make tea, rich in vitamin C

FINDING FOOD SOURCES

Animals may also provide needed food, but hunting them and killing them is a challenge and will use up a great deal of your energy. However, the benefit from eating meat is tremendous, especially in cold weather. The hide of larger animals can also provide clothing, shelter and even tools. If you can bring yourself to eat insects, they will provide much needed protein and save you from having to hunt and kill an animal. Some insects that are edible are listed below:

- Grasshoppers, Locusts, Crickets; they can be roasted or dried, served in soups and stews; catch them at the tops of plants and pick them in the early morning
- Ants; may be roasted, ground into powder and added to stews; find them under rotted stumps or logs; the larger the ant the better
- Grubs and Caterpillars; can be used in soups or stews; some are fuzzy, leave those alone as many are poisonous; Caterpillars usually infest a small area and can be collected and provide several meals
- Reptiles and Amphibians; all snakes and amphibians should be skinned, beheaded and eviscerated before cooking; may be roasted; after catching a rattle snake, bury the head to keep from stepping on it and getting "bitten" by accident; tastes like chicken (it really does, I've eaten it)
- Birds, especially really small birds provide only minimal nourishment and require a lot of energy to catch; however, larger birds such as Chuckers and Turkeys provide a decent meal, so do Sage Hens, Partridges and Quail and these can be herded into traps and won't fly unless pressed too hard; may be roasted over coals or cut up and fried, if you have the means to do so
- Ducks and Geese can be caught while in small ponds by sneaking up on them and using a bow and arrow, made

Continued -

FINDING FOOD SOURCES

- from a strong willow and straight branch for the arrow, using feathers or light and thin shavings of wood for stability of the arrow in flight; this will probably mean you will have to get wet to retrieve the bird
- Fish can be caught with your fish line and hooks; in shallow streams they can even be shot with a barbed arrow that you have attached to your fishing line ... takes some skill here; hooks or barbed arrows can be made out of the wish bone of a small bird and sharpened with your · knife
- Jerky can be made by drying small, thin slices of meet, hanging it over a rack made of green branches of trees; meat doesn't last very well in warm weather, so drying is about your only choice unless you have a great deal of salt or pepper to cover your meat. Flies and other insects will not light on peppered meat & salt will preserve the meat when dried. Squirrels & Rabbits carry diseases, such as Tularemia, so take care when eating them.

FINDING FOOD SOURCES

Animals swift of foot, such as deer, rabbits, elk, and the like, will be difficult to catch without a weapon or some way to snare a rabbit in a trap. Stick to easily caught animals

COOKING IN THE OUT OF DOORS

If water is in short supply, you might consider doing most of your cooking by frying, baking, grilling or roasting. I don't think I need to go into too much detail about how to fry, bake, grill or roast, but I will give some simple basic helpful hints.

Thoroughly cleaning of your food will help in avoiding illness. Removing all entrails and skin and then washing if possible. Wild game should be cooked thoroughly … through and through. Do not eat it rare, or medium rare. Those are luxuries you should avoid in the wild. Meat should be cooked all the way through without any red left in the middle. The same goes for poultry and fish. Cook it 'till it's done, to kill any parasites, germs or worms that might be in the flesh.

Texport Rotisserie Camping Grill

If cooking implements are not available i.e.., frying pans, pots etc., a thick aluminum foil is good for wrapping food in and putting it in the coals. If aluminum foil isn't available, there are still ways of cooking food. Using forked sticks from green (fresh, not dead or dry) branches may also be used by "forking" the meat or vegetable onto the stick, wrapping meat around a stick and even laying it on a rock that has been left in the hot coals and still next to the fire. Hopefully you will be able to secure cooking pots and/or pans to use in the wild. . In any case, when building a camp fire, dig out a depression in the soil beneath and surround it with rocks. This will prevent it from spreading and will also help in maintaining the integrity of the fire by retaining heat.

Outdoor Survival Corner

COOKING IN THE OUT OF DOORS

Kabob

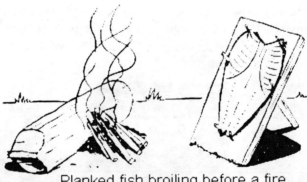

Planked fish broiling before a fire

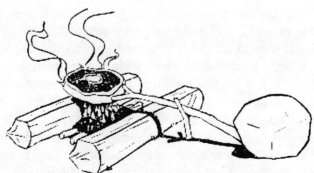

Broiling steak on a green forked stick

COOKING IN THE OUT OF DOORS

Another fine way of cooking out of doors is called "Dutch Oven Cooking." This requires cast iron skillets, pots, pans, grills and the like. These are excellent for cooking on open fires/coals. They are heavy, so you will want to use these only if you are going to be located in the same place for an extended time as you can't pack them around … unless of course you have a packhorse/mule.

This cookware is virtually indestructible and can be placed right on the fire or coals without harming them. They do rust, so they need to be kept dry after use. A rag made out of burlap bag is great for cleaning after use. Try to avoid using water for cleaning. Before using, they have to be conditioned. When shipped from the manufacturer they have a protective coating so you need to heat them up in an oven until they are quite warm and then rub the insides out with paper towels until the towels come out clean.

They hold the heat and can keep food warm for a long time if buried in a hole and covered with dirt. The lid of a cast iron pot is so heavy that it works like a pressure cooker as well. They also heat up quickly and evenly.

In the next few pages I am listing some great recipes for Dutch Oven Cooking taken from a web-site called: www.dream-adventures.com/dutchoven01.html. You will find these recipes scrumpdilyisious:

Outdoor Survival Corner

COOKING IN THE OUT OF DOORS

Wild Boar Roll-Ups

10 slices of bacon

10 thinly sliced pork filets

10 oz. dried apricot halves (cut in small slices)

¾ cup dried cranberries

3 Tbs. honey

1 cup fine breadcrumbs

2 Tbs. dried parsley

1 Tbs. all-purpose flour

1 Tbs. parmesan cheese (finely shredded)

1/2 tsp. sugar

3 tsp. Italian seasoning (mine has paprika, oregano, garlic powder, onion powder and

pepper)

2 Tbs. shortening

2 eggs

10 toothpicks

1 cup apple juice

Don't let this name fool you. It does not have any wild game but this is a serious dish for the pork lover. In a bowl, mix bread crumbs, parsley, flour, cheese, Italian seasoning and sugar. Cut in shortening until mixture is fine crumbs. In a separate bowl mix apricots, cranberries and honey. In another dish beat 2 eggs lightly. Dip one side of the pork filets in the egg mixture and then the crumb mixture. Spoon ¾ cup of apricot mixture onto each pork fillet. Roll fillet (with fruit inside), wrap with a bacon strip and use a toothpick to secure the roll. Place in the bottom of Dutch Oven and add apple juice. Cook for approximately 1 hour at 350 degrees.

COOKING IN THE OUT OF DOORS

Cowboy Shepherd Pie

3 cups ground beef

1 large onion

2 carrots (finely chopped)

2 Tbs. all-purpose flour

1 ¾ cup vegetable stock

Salt and pepper

1 can whole kernel corn (drained)

1 package frozen peas

3 stalkes of celery (finely chopped)

1 pkg. cornbread mix

½ can beer

Pre-cook meat and carrots for 5 minutes. Add celery and all-purpose flour and cook 2 more minutes. Add all other ingredients except cornbread and beer. In a separate bowl, mix cornbread mix and beer. Add on top of other ingredients in Dutch Oven. Cook in DO approximately 45-50 minutes at 325 degrees.

City Slicker (Vegetarian) Beans

1 can white Kidney Beans

1 can red Kidney Beans

¼ tsp. salt and pepper

¾ cup finely chopped sun-dried tomatoes

1 can sliced ripe olives (drained)

1 Tbs. dried oregano

Quick, easy, and tasty dish. Place all ingredients in Dutch Oven and cook approximately 30-40 minutes at 325 degrees.

Outdoor Survival Corner

COOKING IN THE OUT OF DOORS

Grandma's Green Beans

1lb. bacon (cut in 1 inch squares

2 lbs. fresh green beans

1 can mushroom soup

1/4 cup lemon juice

This recipe is like old country cooking, but I get asked to cook it over and over. You can cook the bacon the night before in a skillet and store it in the fridge in a plastic bag. Put all the ingredients in the DO and cook for approximately 35 minutes at 325 degrees.

San Joaquin Fruit Cobbler

Fruit filling

1 box white cake mix

1 cup flour

3/4 can 7-Up (or similar soft drink)

1 Tbsp. cinnamon

Cobblers are great in the Dutch Oven and you can use your favorite fruit filling. My personal favorites are blueberry or cherry. Apricots, peaches, apples and other fruits work just as well. To make clean up easier, first line your DO with aluminum foil. Put the fruit filling in first, then the cake mix and flour, then add 7-Up. Stir lightly so that some of your fruit filling comes upward and 7-Up is mixed with the cake mix and flour. Add cinnamon to the top of the mixture. Cook for approximately 45 minutes at 325 degrees.

If you lined the DO with aluminum foil, clean-up is simple. After the cobbler has been devoured, just lift the aluminum foil out of the DO and most of the mess goes away with it.

Outdoor Survival Corner

COOKING IN THE OUT OF DOORS

Gilroy Chicken Dump

2 elephant garlic bulbs

1 whole chicken (cut up)

6 small potatoes 1 onion (chopped)

10 pearl onions

2 Tbsp. vegetable oil

1 cup chicken stock

2 cups baby carrots

1 cup sliced mushrooms

1/2 tsp. pepper and salt

Thinly slice two elephant garlic bulbs and place in bottom of DO. Place chicken on top of garlic, followed by chopped onions, potatoes and carrots. Place remaining ingredients on top. Cook in DO for approximately 1 hour at 350 degrees

Martha's Favorite (Lemon Asparagus and Baby Carrots)

2 bunches fresh asparagus

1/2 lb. baby carrots

1 Tbsp. lemon juice

1/2 cup chicken broth

1/2 tsp. lemon pepper

Super simple yet a big favorite.

Put all ingredients in DO. Cook

for approximately 35 minutes at

325 degrees.

COOKING IN THE OUT OF DOORS

Dutch Pears To Die For

5-7 Pears
1 cup orange juice
½ cup lemon juice
1 cup water
1/2 to 1 cup sugar
1 cinnamon stick
3 whole cloves (optional)
1 tsp orange rind (optional)

Peel the pears and slice in half. Cook the orange juice, lemon juice, water and sugar with lid off until sugar is dissolved. Then add the cinnamon stick, cloves and orange rind and lay the pears in the bottom of the Dutch Oven. Replace lid and cook for approximately 35 minutes at 325 degrees.

Wagon Train Potatoes

1 cup bacon (cut in 1 inch squares)

3 medium-sized potatoes

1 onion 1 cup cheddar cheese

1/2 bell pepper

1 package frozen green peas

CAMP COOKIN'

You can cook the bacon the night before in a skillet and place in the fridge in a baggie. Thinly slice potatoes and chop onion and bell pepper. Place all ingredients in DO and cook for approximately 35 minutes at 325 degrees. Yummy, yummy, yummy!

Outdoor Survival Corner

COOKING IN THE OUT OF DOORS

Napa Raison Bread Pudding

8 slices cinnamon raisin bread

4 eggs

2 cups milk

1 tsp. vanilla

1/4 cup sugar

1/4 cup butter (melted)

1/2 cup raisons

1 tsp. cinnamon

Cut the bread into 1 inch squares and place in bottom of DO. Mix the remaining ingredients and pour over bread. Replace lid and cook for approximately 50 minutes at 325 degrees.

Keep in mind, this book is to make things simple. Many survival and emergency books I have seen and web-sites I have researched get so complicated with things that it is very discouraging. I don't try to get into very complicated instructions. I use the KISS method: Keep It Simple Stupid.

Outdoor survival is just that ... survival, and if we can do it as simply as possible, we will have less stress and be able to not only help ourselves, but others as well. Be wise as a fox and harmless as a dove.

Enjoy!

FIRST-AID & SANITATION

Refer to the **First Aid Corner** for more detail about first aid. First aid means just that: Aid we give first. You can eliminate the need for first aid treatment while living out of doors by following some simple rules. If we are forced out of doors, it is often because our home is uninhabitable for some reason or another. It may be destroyed, heavily damaged or in an area contaminated or threatened by chemical spills, fire, flood or even war or terrorist attack. Sometimes we have warnings of impending disasters and emergencies and we'll have time to gather up our outdoor gear. Best case scenario, we have time to take what we need with us into the wild.

Some simple rules to follow:

- If you have time and it is possible, lock all doors and board up windows of your home before leaving; secure your valuables and important papers; take spare clothing and some cash with you; take a weapon and ammunition for protection and hunting if you have to hunt; small caliber pistol and rifle for bigger game

- Wear you outdoor clothing and good hiking/walking foot wear when leaving; douse yourself with insect repellent and take it with you; if your neighbors and friends are equally prepared, travel with them, there is safety in numbers … remember, most people will not be prepared; try to set up camp as far away from the disaster or trouble as possible and avoid groups of unprepared people

- If you are on medication, take that with you as well including over the counter medications; First-Aid kit should be part of your outdoor gear

- Be careful when using an axe, hatchet or knife, a cut can turn into a big problem if it gets infected; set up your shelter first and then a fire pit for cooking and warmth;

- Before eating, search out a reliable water source; if water is far away, consider moving camp to your water source; camp in amongst large trees if possible

Outdoor Survival Corner

FIRST-AID & SANITATION

- Sanitation is very important because without it, you can become very ill quickly which will really put you in a bad way; at least 25 yards away from your camp, dig a hole about two feet deep and a foot wide and after each use, cover the waste with soil removed from the hole; when the hole is half full, fill it in and dig another and repeat the process; no need to pour gray water (water from washing and cleaning) into the hole; food scraps will attract animals and all sorts of critters, so digging a hole for scraps might be a good idea … unless wanting to attract them for eating

- Winter time poses a problem for digging, if digging a hole cannot be accomplished, then remove yourself further from your camp when eliminating waste; cover waste with snow after each episode

- Learn to identify poisonous plants that, if touched, cause problems; poison ivy, poison sumac and poison oak are the most frequently encountered plants that cause problems

- Avoid climbing in difficult places to avoid turning an ankle, falling or causing injuries; never physically encounter wild animals, not only from getting bitten or even eaten, but contracting rabies; most animals will run from humans, and if you encounter one that doesn't, it may have rabies so avoid it at all costs ie., foxes, skunks, raccoons, rabbits, coyotes, and bats are often infected

Leaves of three, let them be...

FIRST-AID & SANITATION

This one you can sit on the lower and rest back on the higher. The other one is for pampered survivors. Let it suffice to say, sanitation is paramount for outdoor survival.

It would be wise to have sanitary wipes or hand sanitizer in your gear. I mention the poisonous plants and show their picture so you won't mistakenly use them for toilet paper. That would create a very painful situation, so be careful.

Sanitation is the hygienic means of preventing human contact from the hazards of wastes to promote health. You want to promote health in stressful situations and when you can't get help for an illness. Accidents will happen in the out of doors and cannot be totally prevented, only minimized or mitigated. But one thing you can prevent almost absolutely is staying clean and/or away from human and animal waste and being careful with what you eat and how it is cooked. Keep food covered and away from flies, they carry disease.

FIRST-AID & SANITATION

Flies not only carry diseases, but they can also infect a cut, so be sure to clean your cuts and scrapes thoroughly and keep covered with clean bandages. Antiseptic is a must in your survival gear. Antiseptic comes in many different forms. Alcohol is cheap and easily acquired; Mercurochrome and iodine is as well. A tube of Neosporin is also good to have. Basic First Aid kits will not have too much in them, so get a good kit with more than just the basics. It isn't talked about very often, but the old style feminine sanitary napkins are great for large wounds. Even the new types are good. They are clean and absorb a large amount of blood. Baby diapers for new-borns are also good bandage makers.

Purchase a Boy Scout manual because there are many examples of bandaging and treating wounds with simple illustrations to assist you. Being an Eagle Scout myself, I can't give enough praise to the Scouting program for it taught me many outdoor skills.

The Boy Scout manuals are simple and straight forward; easily understood and applied. The reason for this is obvious; these manuals are written for young boys ages 11-15 so they have to be simple to understand. I finished my scouting in early 1965 but I still have my manual from way back then. The manual was printed in 1952 and is still in very good shape. I have even used some of the illustrations in this book straight out of my old manual. Simple huh?

Outdoor Survival Corner

KNOT TYING FOR SURVIVING OUTDOORS

When I go into the wilds I take this manual with me even today. It is an invaluable tool. Some basic and simple knots will help you tremendously in the wild out of doors. You will have to tie off a rope between two trees to drape a tarp or space blanket over it; you will have to tie a fishing knot; perhaps you will have to lower yourself over a rock ledge or pull a large log for firewood back to camp. Knots are invaluable because they have so many applications. They all have a name and they all have a special purpose. Most people only know how to tie a granny knot or tie shoes with a bow, but any farther … not a chance! One thing you don't want to do is use a knot for the wrong purpose as it may slip or fail and cause injury. Below are some knot tying instructions right from my Boy Scout manual which are easily learned. You will immediately understand for what they are used. So, here we go:

Knot #1 This is the Sheetbend. Works well when tying two ropes together of different sizes and it doesn't require a lot of rope to tie.

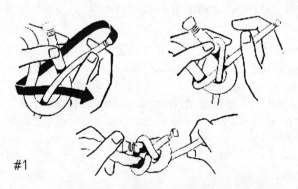

#1

KNOT TYING FOR SURVIVING OUTDOORS

Knot#2   This is the Clove Hitch. Easy to tie and untie. It is used for tying a rope to a peg or stake and will hold even if the peg or stake is slippery/wet, because it pulls against itself. Works well as the starting knot for lashing things together, such as a raft. This can also be tied by making two under hand loops, placing the top loop over the bottom and slipping over the top of the peg or stake and pulling both ends of the rope tight

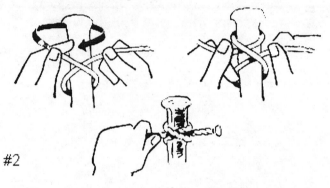

#2

Knot#3   This is the Half Hitch. It is most always used in two's; from this we have "tie two half hitches" around that pole. I wonder if two half hitches make a whole hitch?

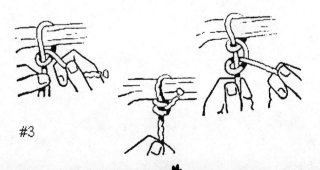

#3

Outdoor Survival Corner

KNOT TYING FOR SURVIVING OUTDOORS

Knot #4   This is the Bowline. It's a little more complex and
needs a little practice, but this is the King of all
knots. Why? Because you have a loop that will
NOT slip. It is important as a rescue knot. It can be
used to tie around a tree, a rock or pole or joining
two ropes together. It is a knot you should learn to
tie blindfolded with one hand, around yourself or
around someone else. It is a knot that once learned,
can be tied very quickly. In Scouts, we used to have
races to see who could tie it the fastest …
practice!

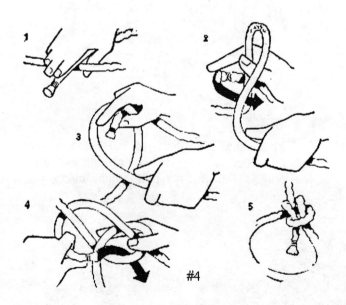

#4

KNOT TYING FOR SURVIVING OUTDOORS

Knot #5   This is the Tautline Hitch. It gets its name because the line must be taught for it to work properly, because when tension is released, the knot becomes loose. Works well for tying tent guy lines with tension. This knot is the same as two Half Hitches, except that there is an extra turn around the standing part, in the direction of the strain or pull.

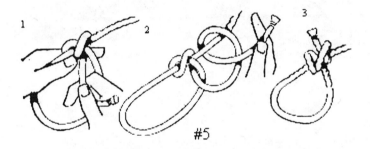

#5

Knot #6   This is the Bowline on a Bight. Used also as a rescue knot because it will have two loops instead of one, allowing a person to slip one leg into each loop while holding on to the rope as it is pulled.

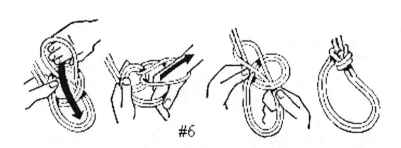

#6

KNOT TYING FOR SURVIVING OUTDOORS

Knot #7   This is a Sheepshank. Has really nothing to do with sheep, but is used primarily for shortening rope. Very useful if you are stringing a rope bridge if the rope droops too much in the middle.

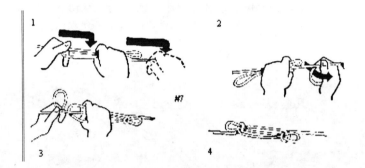

Knot #8   This is the Slip Knot. This is used simply for tying a rope onto something when you need to pull the rope from the other end to tighten it. The knot end allows the rope to slip through the knot as it tightens.

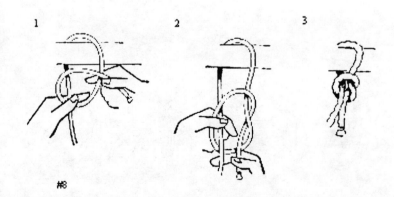

Outdoor Survival Corner

KNOT TYING FOR SURVIVING OUTDOORS

Knot #9   This is the Lariat Loop. Used primarily for a "Cowboy's" rope-to-rope livestock. It has other practical uses such as throwing the rope around something that is out of your immediate reach, or catching a bear, if you have a mind to.

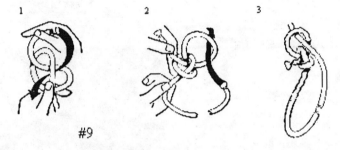

#9

Knot #10   This is the Hitching Tie. This is used to tie something off that you may wish to untie quickly, such as tying off a horse to a hitching post. You simply take the end of the rope out of the last loop and the knot collapses.

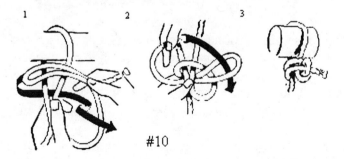

#10

These are the top ten most useful knots and will serve you well while surviving in the out of doors. All you have to do is use them a few times and you will remember them.

Outdoor Survival Corner

KNOT TYING FOR SURVIVING OUTDOORS

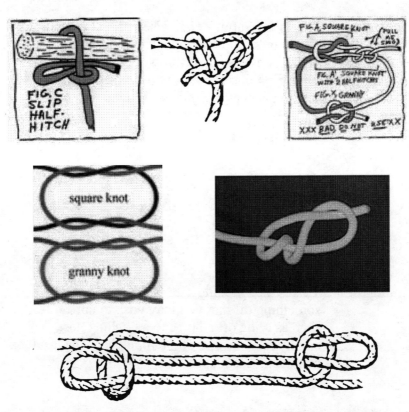

There are so many applications for knots and will serve the knot user well. Have you ever heard the saying that someone (or yourself) needs to learn the ropes? Well, this has to do with seamen having to learn the knots used on vessels at sea. Navy seamen still have to learn knots, even in this modern age.

One last comment for this section: A Monkey's Paw knot is used to wrap a rope around a large steel ball or a rock at the end for seamen to be able to throw the end of the rope to someone standing on the pier or bank or other ship. This rope is usually a small one tied to the very large ropes used at sea to allow the person receiving the Monkey's Paw to pull the very large rope to them.

Outdoor Survival Corner

OUTDOOR SURVIVAL SUMMARY

Ok, let's summarize what we have learned:

- Shelter is the first priority for being out of doors; clothing shelter as well

- Methods of starting fire; matches, magnesium and steel, flint and steel, bow drill; carry plastic baggies of dryer lint or wood shavings

- Locate sources of water; sloping, shaded sides of hills; moist ground; cutting up vegetation and placing in plastic bag; using a clean cloth or bandana and wiping the dew off grass in the early morning

- Precautions using water; store water in your stomach; boiling or straining water to clear out debris and flotsam; stay still and remain in the shade to preserve body fluids; place small pebbles in your mouth to stave off thirst; urinate on your bandana and tie around your neck to cool your body

- Food sources; wild berries; roots. shoots or bulbs from plants; insects; snakes or amphibians; stinging nettle boiled down for tea/ rose hips; wild onions; small critters and birds; dry meat/make jerky to preserve it

- Cooking in the out of doors; build a fire pit with rocks encircling it; cook by using green sticks to wrap or skewer meat; cook all meat well to kill parasites and other · germs; use pots and pans if you have them; learn to use Dutch Oven cooking; try some of the recipes included in this section

- First-Aid & Sanitation; follow safety rules to minimize injury; wear proper clothing and footwear when walking or hiking; be careful using knives, hatchets or axes; dig a sanitation pit; bury food scraps unless trying to attract small critters; learn how to identify poisonous plants that are most common for your area; be sure to add extra bandages and antiseptic ointments and medications and Rx's to your First-Aid kit

Continued -

OUTDOOR SURVIVAL SUMMARY

- Knot tying; learn knots illustrated in this section; knots are very handy and useful in the out of doors; some knots should be learned to be able to tie blindfolded and with one hand; practicing knots a few times is all that's needed to learn them

This **Corner** is probably right up there at the top of importance in this entire book. It is not all encompassing for sure. There are many other outdoor skills that could take up this entire book. For example, reading maps, tracking and stalking game to name a few. This is a book on simple emergency preparedness; to try and stimulate the reader into at least beginning to prepare for an eventuality of having to live out of doors for an extended period of time. Remember, if ye are prepared, ye shall not fear!

Finances in Order Corner

★ $ ★ Finances in Order Corner ★ $ ★

Simple steps to help you in this corner:

1. Find and stick to a budget that works for you
   (you'll be amazed at what you can accomplish)

2. Use worksheets within this corner to figure your annual, monthly and weekly debts.

3. Set aside a budget for a vacation, a new plasma screen TV, or new vehicle. You can do it!

4. Plan a holiday budget and stick to it!

5. Be aware of little expenses, a small leak will sink a ship;
   (bank account fees, coffee fees (the Latte Factor), soda pop (big gulp), etc.

6. Interest never sleeps, pay down credit card debt quickly

7. Remember to keep your emergency preparedness planning within your budget

8. File all Federal, State and Local Taxes to keep in compliance with government agencies

9. Estate planning to protect and preserve assets is an important step for everyone!

10. Keep it simple, don't get overwhelmed and have FUN!

Wise Council

The LDS (Mormon) people have been given wise council for many years to prepare for adversity by having a little money set aside.

Doing so adds immeasurable security and well-being. Every family has a responsibility to provide for its own needs to every extent possible.

Families are encouraged to look to their finances and be aware of their conditions, where ever they live. All are urged to be modest in one's expenditures; to discipline ourselves in our purchases, avoid debt and to pay off debt as quickly as possible.

This will free everyone from bondage. Save a little money regularly to gradually build a financial reserve and use a budget. Keep a record of expenditures. Record and review monthly income and expenses.

Determine how to reduce what is spent on nonessentials. Establish what is spent on food, housing, utilities, insurance, transportation, clothing and so on.

(Please see following Budget Worksheets)

BASIC BUDGETING WORKSHEET

Total Monthly Gross Income	Planned	Actual
-Wages/Salaries (after taxes)	$_____	$_____
-Interest Income	$_____	$_____
-Investment Income	$_____	$_____
-Other Income	$_____	$_____
TOTAL INCOME	$_____	$_____

Expenses

Housing Expenses

	Planned	Actual
Rent or Mortgage	$_____	$_____
Utilities	$_____	$_____
Insurance (divide monthly)	$_____	$_____
Repairs on home	$_____	$_____
Property Taxes (divide monthly)	$_____	$_____

Car Expenses

	Planned	Actual
Loan Payment(s)	$_____	$_____
Gasoline	$_____	$_____
Insurance (divide monthly)	$_____	$_____
Maintenance/Repair	$_____	$_____

Miscellaneous

	Planned	Actual
Church Tithes & Offerings	$_____	$_____
Food Costs (Monthly Groceries)	$_____	$_____
Childcare	$_____	$_____
School Tuition/Supplies	$_____	$_____
Medical/Dental Bills/CoPays	$_____	$_____
Pet Supplies & Vet Exams	$_____	$_____
Entertainment, video rentals, etc	$_____	$_____
Clothing	$_____	$_____
Haircuts	$_____	$_____
Gifts	$_____	$_____
Subscription Dues (newspapers)	$_____	$_____
Association Dues (clubs, homes)	$_____	$_____

Debts

		Planned	Actual
Creditor A_____	Balance _____	$_____	$_____
Creditor B_____	Balance _____	$_____	$_____
Creditor C_____	Balance _____	$_____	$_____
Creditor D_____	Balance _____	$_____	$_____
TOTAL EXPENSES		$_____	$_____

Monthly Surplus or Shortage	Planned	Actual
(Income Less Expenses)	$_____	$_____

ANNUAL BUDGET WORKSHEET

Year _____

This worksheet is used to budget annual expenses, such as insurance (Health, Vehicle, Property, etc.), taxes, capital expenditures, warranties, school tuition, etc. Adjust household budget as needed and keep annual budgeted funds in an interest-bearing savings account or short-term CD if possible. This will help in breaking down and looking at your finances for the over-all year.

Expenses	Approx. Annual Cost Annual	Divide by 12 Monthly
1. Home/Renters Insurance	$_____	$_____
2. Auto Insurance	$_____	$_____
3. Medical/Dental Expense	$_____	$_____
4. Holiday Expense	$_____	$_____
5. Vacation, Travel Expense	$_____	$_____
6. Property Taxes	$_____	$_____
7. Homeowners Dues	$_____	$_____
8. Capital Expenditure #1	$_____	$_____
9. _____	$_____	$_____
10. _____	$_____	$_____
11. _____	$_____	$_____
12. _____	$_____	$_____
13. _____	$_____	$_____
14. _____	$_____	$_____
15. _____	$_____	$_____
16. _____	$_____	$_____
17. _____	$_____	$_____
18. _____	$_____	$_____
19. _____	$_____	$_____
20. _____	$_____	$_____
TOTAL	$_____	$_____

Monthly Amount Needed to Set Aside
$_____

Working Through Debt Worksheet

Use this worksheet to manage your creditors and debts each month. Work towards getting them paid off as quickly as possible. Breaking it down on paper can make this work!

MONTHLY WORKSHEET

Creditors/Debts	Balance	Int. Rate	Finance Charges	Payment Made	Balance
Debt 1 _____	_____	____	_____	_____	_____
Debt 2 _____	_____	____	_____	_____	_____
Debt 3 _____	_____	____	_____	_____	_____
Debt 4 _____	_____	____	_____	_____	_____
Debt 5 _____	_____	____	_____	_____	_____
Debt 6 _____	_____	____	_____	_____	_____
Debt 7 _____	_____	____	_____	_____	_____
Debt 8 _____	_____	____	_____	_____	_____
Debt 9 _____	_____	____	_____	_____	_____
Debt 10 _____	_____	____	_____	_____	_____
Total for Month	_____			_____	_____

Weekly Spending Worksheet

Use this worksheet to manage your spending habits, this will help you keep track of where your money is going each week. If you are spending too much money in one or more categories, try to cut back or adjust in other areas. You can do it! Find out where that pocket money goes.

Monthly Amount Available for Spending $_____

Spending Categories	Week 1	Week 2	Week 3	Week 4	Week 5	Totals
Food:						
Groceries						
Eat Out						
Snacks						
Vitamins						
_____						
Clothing:						
_____						
Entertainment:						
DVD Rentals						
Movies						
Fun Parks						
_____						
Vehicle Expense:						
Gasoline						
Repairs/Maint.						
Trains/Buses,etc						
Household Items:						
_____						
Misc. Items:						
Gifts						
Hobbies						
Books, Cd's						
Magazines						
_____						
TOTALS:						

✳$✳ Finances in Order Corner ✳$✳

Vacation/Get-A-Way Budget Worksheet

Can you afford it? How much money will you have to spend on your vacation or get-a-way, and where will the funds come from?

Income:
Savings
Gifts of Cash _____
Other Income _____
Total Funds to Use: _____

Expenses:
Wardrobe Necessities
Luggage & locks _____
Passport Fees _____
Inoculations/medications _____
Sundries (suntan lotion, etc.) _____
Personal Care (waxing, etc.) _____
Extra pair of glasses, sun glasses, contacts _____
Child care/pet care expense _____
Camera/film/processing _____
Travel:
Airfare _____
Transportation/taxi's,bus,train,ferry, etc. _____
Airport Parking _____
Airport Magazines, snacks, etc. _____
Gasoline if driving _____
Tolls _____
At the Destination: _____
Hotel Expense _____
Breakfast, Lunch, Dinner Expense _____
Beer, Wine, Alcoholic beverages _____
Tips _____
Phone calls, Internet connection _____
Souvenirs, gifts, postcards _____
Activity Fees (horseback riding, golf, spa, etc.) _____
Equipment Rental (snorkel, scuba, golf cart, etc) _____
Excursions Fares _____
Gambling _____
Other _____

TOTAL EXPENSES _____

Holiday Budget Worksheet

What if you could budget over the entire year to help out when the holidays come around. That is such a stressful time and if things were budgeted before hand, you will be able to enjoy the time with family and friends.

Holiday Expense List	Budgeted Cost	Actual Cost
Gifts for Family	_____	_____
Gifts for Friends	_____	_____
Gifts for neighbors, teachers, coworkers, etc	_____	_____
Special Charities	_____	_____
Christmas Cards/Postage	_____	_____
Home Decorations	_____	_____
Christmas Tree & Decorations	_____	_____
Baking Supplies	_____	_____
Gift Wrap/bags/bows,tape,etc	_____	_____
Holiday Food Costs	_____	_____
Party Supplies	_____	_____
Other _____	_____	_____
Other _____	_____	_____
Other _____	_____	_____
TOTAL AMOUNTS	_____	_____

Holiday Gift List (Names)	Gift Ideas	Budget	Actual Cost
1. _____	_____	_____	_____
2. _____	_____	_____	_____
3. _____	_____	_____	_____
4. _____	_____	_____	_____
5. _____	_____	_____	_____
6. _____	_____	_____	_____
7. _____	_____	_____	_____
8. _____	_____	_____	_____
9. _____	_____	_____	_____
10. _____	_____	_____	_____
TOTAL AMOUNTS (add to list above)		_____	_____

★ $ ★ $ ★ $ ★ $ ★ $ ★ $ ★ $ ★ $ ★ $ ★ $ ★

Some Simple Thoughts on Finances

Here are some interesting thoughts from the Poor Richard's Almanac:

There are no gains without pains
Diligence is the mother of good luck
One today is worth two tomorrows
If you would be wealthy, think of saving as well as getting
Fools make feast and wise men eat them
He that has a trade, has an estate
Wink at small faults; remember thou hast great ones
If you would reap praise you must sow the seeds, gentle words and useful deeds
Think of these three things; Whence you come, Where you are going, and to whom you must account
Fear to do evil and you need fear nothing else
Wish not so much to live long as to live well
Lend money to an enemy and you will gain him, to a friend and you will lose him
Beware of little expenses, a small leak will sink a great ship!

Some thoughts on how to save on the bottom line:

Starting with basics:
Choose the best place to stash your cash. If it's in a bank, find one that does not charge fees for your accounts. There are many out there. Just that alone will save on the bottom line at least $100.00

The Latte Factor:
We all waste five to ten dollars a day on little things, such as money for a cup of coffee, a pastry, soda, candy bars, and a dollar here and there adds up over a year. You could take that money and put it to better use for you.

Get Organized:
Keep on track of how much you're spending throughout the year.

Some Simple Thoughts on Finances

Myself, being an accountant, I keep receipts for everything. If you're not used to saving receipts you could set that as a short-term goal. Buy a small filing cabinet or have just one place in your home such as a large drawer where all your receipts can go. Get a notebook and organize with plain paper, your individual worksheets on budgets, goals (short-term and long-term), etc. If you right something down it seems to connect with the brain so much easier and the thoughts become yours. Figure out a way to SAVE, SAVE, SAVE...Know that one credit card is enough and avoid debt like the plague. Remember we're in bondage with interest hanging over our heads.

Some additional thoughts:

> Make a weekly or monthly financial budget. Identify what your basic costs and extra expenses are.
> Avoid impulse spending and try to limit purchases to necessities.
> Do your best to pay credit cards in full each month.
> Leave credit cards at home when shopping to help stick to your budget.
> Research before you buy any major purchases. You can save money if you know where or how to get the best deal.
> Never spend more than a hundred dollars on anything without taking forty-eight hours to think it over. You can give yourself the chance to decide if the purchase is really necessary.
> Trim expenses where you can, remember that something is not a treat if done on a daily basis. If you eat out frequently, try to go out one night a week, or use public transportation one day a week or bring a sack lunch instead of purchasing one.
> Buy the car you need instead of the car you want. There is so much more involved with insurance, taxes, repairs, maintenance and fuel. Be careful and shop wisely.
> Set short-term and long-term financial goals. If you don't set goals, you'll turn around one day and wonder, what

Some Simple Thoughts on Finances

happened to your life. Set short-term goals for vacations, a new car or boat, etc. Set Long-term goals for children's college funds, retirement goals, investments, etc.

Some Retirement Planning Mistakes:

➢ Putting college savings ahead of retirement savings. Nobody will loan you money for retirement, however, they will for kids' college expenses.
➢ Thinking that it's too late to start saving for retirement. You may be surprised at how aggressively you can save.
➢ Not contributing enough to a 401(k) plan to get the full company match.
➢ Withdrawing money from a retirement plan, whether borrowing or prematurely cashing out really hurts the pocket book at tax time. You pay an additional 10% penalty for early withdrawal.
➢ Basing retirement income needs on your current income rather than your anticipated expenses
➢ Not using tax advantaged savings plans. Uncle Sam offers you breaks. Use them.
➢ Not updating retirement plan with current beneficiary information.

Only 4 in 10 Americans have tried to estimate how much money they will need in retirement, according to the Employee Benefit Research Institute. Online tools and financial planners can help in this overwhelming task.

Some useful Financial Websites are:
www.quicken.com (includes info on investing, banking, retirement, taxes and insurance
www.mutuals.com (lists practically every mutual fund there is)
www.morningstar.com (includes a retirement center and investing classroom)
There are also many websites out there that offer free budget worksheets of all sorts, just surf the net.

✱ $ ✱ Finances in Order Corner ✱ $ ✱

Estate Planning Information

In today's world, what with easy credit, investment scams, high and confiscatory taxes, taxes while living and after death, it is paramount that we have our finances in order.

Placing one's finances in order need not be overwhelming. This *Corner* is not to give investment advice or how to get out of debt or even how to arrange one's financial affairs. Rather, this *Corner* is to make suggestions as to what one should arrange, plan and have created/set up to assist in times of personal tragedy or the death of a loved one.

311

Estate Planning Information

Go to the ant...consider her ways, and be wise: which having no guide, overseer, or ruler, provideth her meat in the summer, and gathereth her food in the harvest.

How long wilt thou sleep...? When wilt thou arise out of thy sleep?"

Proverbs 6:6-9

This Chapter is not meant to give any kind of financial advice as to what constitutes a good investment or where one should go to invest one's money. We mean merely to remind or make suggestions that one could consider when making decisions as to getting one's finances in order.

Consider this: What if our debit cards or credit cards were no longer accepted, due to some financial crisis? What if the banks were no longer accepting checks and/or paper currency? Plan for the worst, expect the best. If this nation has a financial meltdown, is your house in order, financially?

Estate Planning Information

We have all heard the phrase, "Never leave home without it." We should never leave this world (home) without an Estate Plan.

Like most of us, we put things off, and Estate Planning is one of those things we, as Americans, put off until it is too late. This procrastination can and will have a devastating affect on our families.

Estate Planning Information

However, a comprehensive Estate Plan is one thing that can protect your assets, ensure that your wishes are carried out and support those left behind.

A comprehensive Estate Plan consists of 2 parts:

1. The Death Plan
2. The Life Plan

Death Plan = Avoid Probate

- Minimize or Avoid Estate and Inheritance Taxes

Life Plan = Prepare for incapacity

- Guard against creditors and predators
- Controlled and protected distributions of cash or other property/assets

If something should happen to you, there are many factors that can greatly reduce the value of your estate and leave less of what you intended to your heirs:

- Statutory probate fees; beginning in some states- as low as $46,000 gross estate

- Exorbitant medical bills due to long term care

- Creditors and predators forcing the sale of assets

- The fact that most assets in the estate are not readily liquid and have to be sold for much less than their true value

A properly structured Integrated Estate Plan (IEP) will safeguard against such circumstances and help to keep these and other factors from unnecessarily decreasing the value of the estate

Estate Planning Information

A well structured IEP will also ensure the proper fulfilling of the decedent's wishes, allow for fair and equitable distribution of cash/assets without the worry of a larger portion of the estate being sacrificed and give peace of mind to the family. During a time of bereavement, the one thing family members don't need, are additional worries about how to deal with the estate.

An Integrated Estate Plan will, of necessity, require the creation of a Trust, or Trusts. The creation of a Trust must be handled with great care and certain provisions must be written into the Trust Instrument for maximum protection of the estate. A very good source for an IEP is Farr West Business Consulting and Estate Planning and can be reached through their website at: www.farrwestbusiness.com

Avoidance of probate, asset protection, and the mitigation or complete avoidance of estate and/or inheritance tax is only part of a good IEP.

A good IEP will include a Will, but a stand alone Will does not avoid probate or the diminution of the estate through taxes on the estate and/or on the heirs of the estate.

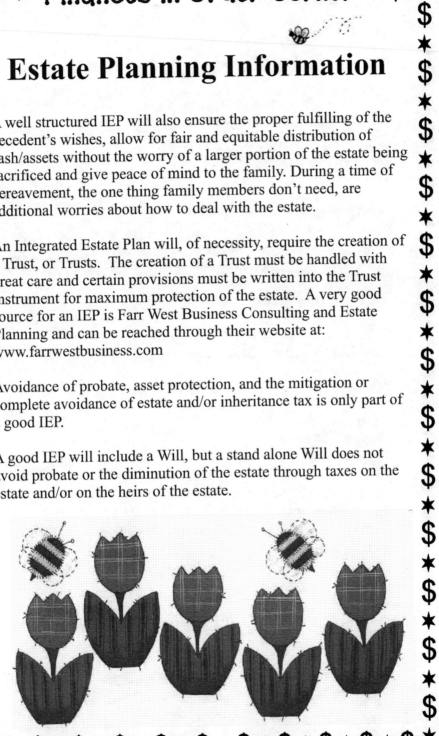

FAQ's & Questions

- What happens if one dies without a Will?

- What happens if one or more of one's heirs pre-deceases the Testator?

- What happens to certain "sentimental assets that perhaps only one heir wants?

- How does one's death effect taxes for the and/or heirs?

- How is a Trustee or Executor chosen?

- What happens to assets left out of one's Estate Plan/Trust by accident or neglect?

- Can one change one's mind after the IEP is created?

- And many more ???

Financial planning is an integral part of estate planning. A good financial plan is designed to take care of your life planning needs, and the Estate Plan is designed to take care of your needs and fulfill your wishes after death. The above questions will be answered in as simple a manner as possible in the following pages.

Additional Estate Planning Comments

If one dies without a Will, the estate of the decedent will most likely be probated. "Probate" comes from the word Probation. Essentially, this means the decedent's estate will be held in limbo/probation until the state decides who gets what. Not so good! Once probate is finished, the next of kin will then have claim to the estate.

The problem with having an estate probated, is the statutory cost, which can be substantial. Many times the heirs must sell a sizeable portion of the estate to pay the expenses of probate and taxes. And usually the sale is a quick sale at much less than FMV. An IEP will will prevent this from happening.

A well formed Trust will provide for the possibility of an heir (Beneficiary) dying before the Trustor (the one who had the Trust created) by making provisions for transference of beneficial interests to the surviving heirs. One of the great benefits of a Trust over a stand alone will, is the ease of changing or disinheriting heirs. Sentimental assets one wishes to leave to certain heirs are provided for in a Will, or a Trust with a "List of Particulars" which will be attached to, or included in a Pour Over Will.

Basically, a Pour Over Will is a will that is included in an IEP which says that anything left out of "my" Trust by neglect, procrastination or by time constraints is deemed to be "poured over into the Trust.

If an estate is large enough (>$2M in 2008) there will be estate taxes to pay. The tax is paid by the estate. The estate tax return must be filed within 9 months of the decedent's death. Therefore, there isn't really much time to sell some assets, as in real estate.

Much time is used up in bereavement, funeral, paying debts of the estate and decedent, filing of insurance claims etc.

Additional Estate Planning Comments

So, this means the heirs will usually have to sell off assets of the estate to pay the taxes. In the case of real estate and investments, the value over the years has grown, creating another tax to the estate or heirs...capital gains tax.

A Trustee, Executor or Personal Representative is usually chosen from a trusted friend or family member. Selection of a Trustee in an Estate Plan will normally be the same individual chosen as Executor or Personal Representative. However, while the Testator or Trustor is yet living, or at least one of the spouses is yet alive, they will fill the position as Trustee and select someone as personal representative or successor Trustee of the Trust.

There are professional Trustee servicing companies in most cities, however they are costly, usually an annual percentage of the estate value as a fee. A family member or trusted friend is preferable in most cases.

A Pour Over Will provides for assets left out of an estate plan/Trust by accident, neglect or time constraints. See prior page for a more detailed explanation.

A well formed IEP will have provisions to enable the changing one's mind, adding theirs/Beneficiaries or eliminating same.

Keep in mind that an estate consists not only your home, cars, cash, stocks, bonds, and other real and tangible property, but your retirement (not SS benefits and some other government or sub-government retirement plans), and face value of your life insurance as well.

★ $ ★ Finances in Order Corner ★ $ ★

Additional Estate Planning Comments

Married couples can usually eliminate federal estate taxes entirely at the death of the first spouse through a carefully considered plan capitalizing on the combination of the unlimited marital deduction coupled with the unified credit.

The marital deduction is provided through what is called a Bypass Trust, commonly known as the A-B Trust. This is a Trust arranged and designed to give the surviving spouse full use of the family's economic wealth, while at the same time minimizing, to the extent possible, the total federal estate tax payable at the deaths of both spouses. This is a wonderful planning tool.

The marital deduction is a deduction for gift or estate tax purposes for property passing to (or in a qualifying Trust for) a spouse.

The unified credit is a credit provided to each citizen or resident of the U.S., which can be applied against either gift taxes or estate taxes. (the giver of the gift pays the gift tax, not the receiver)

Unified credit used for gift taxes reduces the amount available for estate taxes. The amount of the unified credit is much less for gift taxes than for estate taxes.
Often, people are "advised" to "gift away" their estate, using up the credit year by year. Not the best approach.

The goal typically is to avoid "over qualification" of the estate for the marital deduction because of "underutilization of the unified credit in the estate of the first spouse to die.

The estate tax unified credit (there is no estate tax in 2010, so that's the best year to die) is scheduled to increase each year. The table is on the next page:

★ $ ★ $ ★ $ ★ $ ★ $ ★ $ ★ $ ★ $ ★ $ ★ $ ★ $ ★

319

✶$ ✶ Finances in Order Corner ✶$ ✶

Additional Estate Planning Comments

Year	Unified Credit	Applicable Credit Amount
'04-'05	555,800	1,500,000
'06-'08	780,800	2,000,000
2009	1,455,800	3,000,000
2010	N/A	N/A
2011 +	345,800	1,000,000

Keep in mind, the estate tax returns goes to 55% in 2011. At this writing, there is much pressure from the democrats in Congress to rescind the high exemption now in place ($2,000,000 and $3,000,000 in 2009) and put the exemption (Applicable Credit Amt) down to $1,000,000 and 55%.
For now, and 2009, the rate is 45%.

A second to die life insurance policy is one way to assist in the payment of taxes.

★ $ ★ Finances in Order Corner ★ $ ★

Important Information

If you are self employed, and/or running your business out of your home you are exposing your family or personal assets to any unforseen liability which might arise.

There also may be some very beneficial tax advantages you are not availing yourself of by being a sole proprietor. In today's litigious climate, predators are always on the lookout for opportunistic events to sue.

Therefore, it behooves everyone to consider doing business as a small business corporation (S-Corp) or as a Limited Liability Company (LLC).

Both an S-Corp and an LLC offer liability protection to the owners. That is, against the owners' personal assets. The cost of doing business in this manner is minimal and cheap insurance against would be predators, looking to get rich at your expense.

Doing business as an S-Corp or LLC does offer other distinct advantages as well.

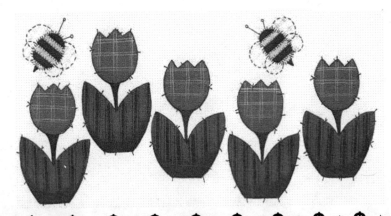

Index

Index

Index

Index

Index

Index

Other Books available through Crockett's Corner

Wheat Cookin`Made Easy

Garden Veggie Cookin`Made Easy
COMING SOON

Whole Grain Cookin`Made Easy
COMING SOON

Food Storage Cookin`Made Easy
COMING SOON

For any information regarding these books of fun recipes, please contact
Crockett's Corner
PO Box 508
Huntsville, UT 84317
(801)745-5662 ,(801) 745-6009 fax
crockettscorner.com (website)
pam@crockettscorner.com (e-mail)

Country Cookin`Made Easy
COMING SOON